THE FIRST

BLACK
QUARTERBACK

MARLIN BRISCOE'S JOURNEY

TO BREAK THE COLOR BARRIER

AND START IN THE NFL

"Best wishes"
Marlin Briscoe '68
#15 Q.B. Broncos
17-0 #86 Dolphins
'72 - '74

The First Black Quarterback

Marlin Briscoe with Bob Schaller

ISBN 1-929478-32-1

Cross Training Publishing
317 West Second Street
Grand Island, NE 68801
(308) 384-5762

This book is manufactured in the United States of America.

Library of Congress Cataloging in Publication Data in Progress.

Published by Cross Training Publishing,
317 West Second Street
Grand Island, NE 68801

Photo Credits: © Clarks Studio

ACKNOWLEDGEMENTS

I want to thank my mother, Geneva, a single mother who sacrificed her personal life to raise my sister and me and who gave us the tools to stand up to the challenges of life and be strong. I want to thank my beautiful sister, Beverly, who was always so much stronger than me.

I want to thank my beautiful daughters, Angela and Rebecca, whom I love dearly. They may not know it, but they helped me the most during my darkest days by inspiring me to not give up, to get my life back together so I could to make them proud of me.

I would like to thank my cousin Bob Rose, my father figure who taught me lessons about sports and about life. He was my mentor, my idol and my source of strength. I would like to thank the late Al Caniglia, my tough but fair football coach at Omaha University.

I would like to thank the people of my church, the First Presbyterian Church, especially Ruth Hirschman and the late Dolores Wilson, for giving me a spiritual home, when I got out of jail.

I would like to thank Roy Roberts, executive director of the Watts/Willowbrook Boys and Girls Club in Los Angeles, who gave me my current job helping kids realize the same dream I had. Roy gives those kids a safe haven from the troubled streets.

I would like to thank Jim Mountain, a big old Irish teddy bear of a man who has gone out of his way to be a special friend over the past few years.

I would like to thank another Irishman—or Irishwoman— Omaha World-Herald sportswriter Colleen Kenney, who was the first to write the story of my descent into drugs and recovery. Three years ago, she worked hard to convince me my story was important to tell because it could inspire other addicts to not give up. Her story brought me out of the mothballs and let people know that I was alive, clean, and back to the Marlin Briscoe they remembered. Her contributions included the stories about my drug days, my life in the fast lane, my "little hustle," and my kidnapping.

I would like to thank author Bob Schaller for his patience and dedication to getting this story out and getting it right.

Most of all, I want to thank God, who makes all things possible. He was my shepherd through the wolves. In my darkest days, He gave me light. He gave me my life back. He was my quarterback. I may have been 17-0 with the Miami Dolphins. But the only game plan that is perfect is God's plan for us.

PREFACE

The man who had won a big battle in the fight for racial equality was close to becoming just another statistic in the war on drugs.

So many stories were circulating about what happened to Marlin Briscoe, as a group of sportswriters talked a few years ago in a newsroom about the man who had been the first African-American to start at, and be the regular, quarterback for a professional football team.

"Dead of a drug overdose in Denver, I think," one said.

"Shot and killed in Los Angeles or New Jersey," reported another.

Actually, both were wrong, though there was a sliver of truth in each. Briscoe's drug problem had taken him to panhandling and living on the street, during which time he had a loaded gun pointed at his head.

After getting his life in order and kicking drugs—with the help of such notable NFL alumni as San Diego Hall of Fame receiver Lance Alworth and former Raiders coach and Buffalo Bills quarterback Tom Flores—a physically fit and cleaned-up Briscoe had slipped, basically unnoticed, back into society, coaching Keyshawn Johnson ("incorrigible," says Briscoe) and Isaac Bruce ("a great young man") in junior college.

He emerged to be honored by the Buffalo Bills in 2001. He also had been inducted into the Hall of Fame for, South High School, and the statewide sports Hall of Fame in Nebraska. He was in the original class of those inducted into the University of Nebraska-Omaha Hall of Fame in 1975.

With the Denver Broncos, Briscoe set a rookie record of 14 touchdown passes in 1968, a record that stands to this day, although Briscoe started just seven games and played in 11, all as quarterback.

From his experiences as the first black starting quarterback, to making the transition to wide receiver for the Bills the next year—and leading the AFC in receiving the next season, despite having never played receiver, even in college—Briscoe's story needed to be told in its entirety, including his role on the two Super Bowl winning teams in Miami, including the NFL's only perfect season.

Though his story of overcoming drugs is probably timely in today's world, it is the personal stories of his career, from a bogus shoplifting arrest in Denver to a confrontation with Al Davis when Briscoe made the Pro Bowl, that are timeless. Briscoe's relationship with Jack Kemp, who would become a vice presidential candidate in 1996, saved Briscoe's NFL career. Briscoe was also with the Bills when James Harris was drafted, becoming the second black to start, and ironically one of his favorite targets was Briscoe. Some are stories that no one has heard, and that's why Briscoe's story is so well worth telling.

Gary Anderson, sports information director at the University of Nebraska-Omaha, Omaha University when Briscoe attended it, said he will never forget "Marlin the Magician."

"The big thing you need to get in this book is that Marlin was not just about sports, because he was the first black in our student government and participated in a lot of social issues," said Anderson, who was on the college paper when Briscoe played. "But he certainly left a legacy in sports here. He was the best football player I've ever seen here, bar none. No one else was even close—and we had some good ones, many who went to the NFL. Marlin was just in a class by himself because his football instincts made him just tremendous. He was ahead of his time by 20 or 30 years. If he played today, he'd be in the Hall of Fame as a quarterback. Marlin was 5-foot-10, but that wouldn't matter today. Doug Flutie is good, but he doesn't have Marlin's athletic ability or arm strength. And today, it wouldn't matter that Marlin is black."

Although Briscoe broke his neck at Omaha University and was told he would never play any sport again, he still passed his physical for the Vietnam draft—a week before his senior season, and was told he would never play any sport again, only after having his childhood dream of playing for the University of Nebraska Cornhuskers go unfulfilled.

"Honestly," Anderson said, "I don't know how Nebraska ever overlooked him. They missed something special. He could have been phenomenal for them."

When Edwin Pope of the Miami Herald interviewed Marlin in Los Angeles in January of 2002 about this book, Pope talked about how Marlin was in such great shape, and looked like he still could play. "The only difference is the snow on top," Pope said, referring to the gray in Marlin's hair.

"I think he has a great story to tell," said Dave Hyde, columnist for the South Florida Sun-Sentinel.

With the eventual—and overdue—proliferation of black quarterbacks in the NFL, including Doug Williams, Warren Moon, Randall Cunningham, Donovan McNabb, Kordell Stewart, Steve McNair, Daunte Culpepper, Aaron Brooks, Shaun King, Quincy Carter, Akili Smith, Michael Vick, Jeff Blake and several others, the timing seemed just right for everyone to learn about Briscoe's journey to the top of the world in breaking a color barrier, followed by a plunge to the depths of society living from high to low.

Marlin wanted to title the book, "Third and Long" to reflect the cliffs that he tiptoed along for a good chunk of his adult life, on the field and off. And that might be a good title if this book is adapted to film be it television or otherwise.

In the end, *The First Black Quarterback* simply summed it up too well. This book chronicles the journey of a man possessed by a desire and talent that took the sporting world by storm but left his personal life in shambles before he rebuilt it. Now, the project manager of a youth center in Watts, California, Briscoe is helping young people, something he has wanted to do since becoming an education major in college.

And with this book, he hopes that people of any age and race can learn from, and enjoy, the long, winding road that has been the life of Marlin Briscoe.

INTRODUCTION

By James Harris,
the "second black (starting) quarterback,"
current Pro Personnel Director, the Baltimore Ravens

He was sweating and breathing hard.

A phone call had come from a man, telling me that Marlin Briscoe was in the hands of drug dealers.

"I think Marlin's dead, and he almost got me killed!" the man said.

But there came Marlin, about 30 pounds lighter than his playing days, to my door, after escaping from a kidnapping related to a drug debt.

"I think the guy is dead!" Marlin said, heavy circles under his eyes.

"No, he just called, and he's not dead," I said.

"That guy almost got me killed!" Marlin said.

"Yes, and he said the same thing about you," I told Marlin.

I was just glad Marlin was alive. That was during Marlin's dark years of drug addiction.

As a college player, I had followed the impressive numbers Marlin had put up as a quarterback at Omaha University—obviously I was especially interested because we're both black. I also followed him from afar during my senior year at Grambling, when Marlin joined the Denver Broncos and became the first black quarterback to start for a professional football team.

When I joined Marlin with the Buffalo Bills in 1969—I started the first game that year, as a rookie—I was glad to see him join our team late in camp. I had heard he was not in the mix to play quarterback in Denver, and they had let him go.

I related to Marlin right away because we had so much in common. He was a great help to me because of his experience in Denver. He also shared with me his frustration with how things were handled in Denver. All Marlin wanted was an opportunity to compete at quarterback. He came to Buffalo bitter about that experience, but eager to fit in and find a place on the team.

Marlin was the only guy on the Bills who understood what I was going through, especially after I was pulled as the starter. The other black players had to worry about competing for their own jobs, so they didn't understand my situation as well as Marlin. He was intelligent and really understood the game—a lot of knowledge for a guy who had just one year in pro ball at that time.

When I was released before the start of the next season, Marlin left camp and came to visit me, because he understood what I was going through, and how it had been handled, not unlike what he went through in Denver. He had really been pulling for me because of his own experience. I don't think the other guys on the team understood it like Marlin did. And that he came to see me was special. He also extended himself to other players who were cut.

The irony with Marlin is this: He was an All-Pro receiver, yet he didn't have the size or speed, although he had outstanding quickness, to play receiver. In other words, he didn't fit the prototype for receivers. So the criteria said there was no way he would succeed. That he did succeed is testimony to the kind of competitor that he is. And the irony is that he was deemed too small to play quarterback. Why was he allowed to compete at receiver—a position he had never played—even though he didn't meet the "requirements" and yet he didn't get that same chance at quarterback?

Over the years, Marlin and I continued to be close, and were neighbors in Los Angeles. He's always been a great friend and a great person.

He struggled with drugs when he left football. I knew Marlin was capable of straddling the line with the partying and those things. But I never thought Marlin would end up succumbing to anything, much less drugs, because he was so strong-willed. When we were neighbors, I'd see a lot of cars at his house. When I'd go visit him, he'd never have drugs or anything out in plain view. He didn't want me exposed to that. When I realized that he had a serious drug addiction and was out of control, it hurt me more than anything else did.

Several former teammates came to talk to Marlin at his house, trying to help him get out of the tailspin. A.J. Martin, another teammate, went with me to talk to Marlin. When I walked back to my house that night, I realized Marlin was in trouble.

It also surprised and bothered me. I ended up realizing that

Marlin was in a struggle to defeat a foe that any competitor would have a hard time beating—drugs. That period frustrated all of us who care for him. We had been so proud of him because all he had gone through to break the color barrier and then learn—and excel at—a new position.

The last time I went to his house, I saw all of these test tubes and other pharmaceutical paraphernalia.

"What's going on?" I asked. "Are these other people chemists or something?"

Soon the other cars disappeared.

Marlin was in over his head. The money was gone and so were his "friends." We all tried to help him initially.

But Marlin had to help himself.

When he came by my house that night after the weekend-long kidnapping, we talked about where he was going to go from there. He went to my room and slept that night. I sat down and called Paul Warfield, a teammate and great friend of Marlin's from his days in Miami.

"Don't give him any money," Paul told me. We had talked about this at length several times, and Paul had even flown across the country to sit down with Marlin and straighten him out.

"We can't help him," Paul told me on the phone that night as Marlin slept, "until he decides he'll help himself. We're doing him more harm than good by giving him money. Give me another call and let me know how things turn out."

Marlin hadn't eaten that whole weekend, as he was held at gunpoint to pay a drug debt. I gave him some money for food.

Those experiences touched me deeply—just seeing him go through that whole trying period of his life.

Marlin disappeared again for several years.

I had talked to Joe Gilliam, who was going through similar problems. All that we—the black quarterbacks—had ever wanted was a chance to play. Our dreams were no different than those of black running backs and receivers. But the black quarterbacks of that era were measured by different standards.

I know that I could have fallen into that same hole.

But I didn't enter the league like Marlin and Joe, thinking all I had to do was perform. Because before I was drafted, my coach at Grambling, Eddie Robinson, told me words I'd never forget.

Don't expect it to be fair.

I lived by those words. Marlin and Joe thought it was not fair, but that it should be fair. Sure, it should be, but it wasn't. I just accepted the fact that it wouldn't be fair, no matter what. I had to leave that part of it behind and not take it with me.

The bitterness and frustration affected Marlin's attitude toward life. Yet he was still able to become one of the best receivers in the game at that time. Still, the hurt was there, because he knew that, even at his size, he was as good as many of the quarterbacks playing.

I was sad to see him take that detour into drugs. But when he finally decided to take the problem on, he beat it. I have never met a competitor like Marlin, so when he wanted to get clean, he did.

Seeing him get to the point now where he's working and doing meaningful things with young people makes me so happy.

He got himself back on the right track.

FOREWORD

By Don Shula, former Head Coach, Miami Dolphins

Even while Marlin Briscoe struggled to overcome his personal problems, I had faith that he would come around.

From the time I brought him to Miami, I saw a lot of good characteristics in Marlin as a person. As he battled through his post-football career problems, I had hope that he would make it back to society.

Of course, we never know that they will turn it around until they step forward and actually do it. I had seen enough of Marlin to know that he is a very bright individual, and if he put his mind to something, he could beat it.

Marlin has come back to be a positive influence in society, and on children, which is something I believe to be very important.

I brought Marlin Briscoe to the Miami Dolphins prior to the 17-0 season of 1972 because he was such a gifted all-around athlete. I knew he could catch the ball. And I knew that he'd be good at running and gaining more yards after he caught it. I really saw him as a big-play receiver. I knew that because he had played so well for Buffalo when our Miami teams would play the Bills. We had a hard time defending Marlin.

We needed a receiver to complement Paul Warfield. With Marlin on one side and Paul on the other, it was hard to defend our team because we had talent on both sides.

Marlin writes in this book that I showed a lot of courage in sticking with him after Marlin had made a mistake that cost us a touchdown, and nearly the game, in the Super Bowl. But I learned a long time ago as a person, and as a coach, that people make mistakes.

If it's a mistake that can't be corrected—or one a person won't correct—then we have to make a decision. But if it's a mistake that can be fixed, and will be fixed, there's no sense in condemning someone for an unintentional miscue.

That was the case with Marlin, in football and in life. Marlin was a dependable player for a long time, just as he was a dependable person for most of his life as he is now.

But his mistake in the Super Bowl didn't cost us the game or cost Marlin his career. His mistakes after his career, fortunately, did not cost him his life.

He pushed forward, as we all should. Now that he's on the right path once again, his lesson is one from which a lot of people can learn.

CONTENTS

Preface by Bob Schaller   5
Introduction by James Harris   9
Foreword by Don Shula   13

1. 17-and-0   17
2. Humble Beginnings   21
3. Encountering Racism   29
4. The "Magic Box"   39
5. Breaking a Barrier   53
6. Broken Neck, Shattered Dreams   67
7. Creating a Place for History in Denver   79
8. Bogus Arrest Threatens Path   91
9. Conspiracy Derails Denver Journey   105
10. Fleeing to Canada, and then New Life in Buffalo   111
11. Telling Al Davis "No"   133
12. Behind the Scenes with the Perfect '72 Dolphins   147
13. A Chance Encounter with Joe Gilliam   159
14. Rozelle Lawsuit Makes Me a Nomad   165
15. The Darkness of Drugs   175
16. Kidnapped by Gang-bangers   183
17. A Bad Trade: Super Bowl Rings for Drugs   189
18. Tom Flores Offers Rehab   197
19. After Prison a Fresh, Clean Start   201
20. The O.J. Simpson Murder Trial   209
21. "1-0"   213
22. The Changing Landscape of the NFL   217

1

17-and-0

"17-and-0."

That was my nickname on the street, a nickname born out of the 1972 Miami Dolphins' perfect, undefeated Super Bowl season.

"Hey, look who's coming," the drug dealers would cackle. "Look at him. It's 17-and-0."

I didn't care, as long as they gave me drugs. I'd go huddle with the other dirty addicts in some crack house or hotel room filled with people and get high.

After I retired from the NFL in 1977, nine years after becoming the first black quarterback to start a game, drugs brought me down. One drug—cocaine—slowly began to control me. Over the course of one lost decade, from about 1978 to 1990, cocaine nearly consumed me. I lost my family. I lost my money. I lost my good name. I went to jail twice.

People who had known me at the top of my game were stunned when they saw me hit rock bottom—clothes hanging from my bony body, eyes glazed over, mouth spouting excuses for why I needed to hit them up for a few bucks.

Only a few close friends knew how to find me during the last few drug years because I didn't want to be found. I was too ashamed. I was too hooked. As much as I had wanted to overcome the race barrier and play quarterback in the NFL, as much as I had wanted to make it as a receiver or win Super Bowls, as much as I had wanted to be a good role model for kids … I wanted that next "hit" of crack even more.

And "17-and-0" got me a lot of crack.

"Excuse me, sir. I'm not a robber or anything," I'd say. "My name is Marlin Briscoe. I was quarterback for the Broncos back in '68. I was on that 17-0 Miami team.

"Well, I'm having a little car problem, and I left all my money at home. Think you could loan me 10 or 20 bucks to fix my hose?"

I always chose men. I didn't want to threaten women. Plus, I figured that men, especially those around my age, were more likely to know me.

They'd look me up and down.

"You're Marlin Briscoe?" they'd say. "You're an ex-NFL player and you look like you weigh 135 pounds. I need to check your story."

So I'd pull out my driver's license and my NFL identification card. And I'd always just happen to have a briefcase in my trunk full of photos of me in my playing days. I'd ask if they wanted one.

"Want me to sign it, too?"

We'd talk football. They'd relax. Then I'd have them look under the car hood and see that what I was saying was true. It was true, with a twist. My car was broken down. But it was broken down because instead of paying to get it fixed, I had spent all my money on drugs.

"You're going to need more than 20 bucks to fix that hose," they'd say, smiling as they reached into their wallets.

"Here, Marlin. Here's a hundred."

I thrived that way. I called it "my little hustle." It was an ongoing hustle because I had to have drugs all day. Most of the time, I was working. I could always get a job. I just couldn't keep a job. I'd show up late or come to work high, and soon I'd be back out hustling again.

I usually kept my own apartment. But some nights, when I hadn't paid the rent, my bed would be in a seedy hotel room or a men's shelter. And once in a while, my bed would be on the streets, my head resting against a cold alley wall.

When I'd awake, my first thought would be drugs.

For drug money, I went to the places throughout Los Angeles where people had money. Different places each time. Golf courses. Grocery stores. Gas stations. I did my little hustle in broad daylight. I knew that early in morning or late at night, people were less likely to trust me.

Nobody called the police or ran away. No one felt threatened. That says something about how good of a hustle I had, because on the mean streets of LA, and even on the trendy streets, you don't trust anybody.

When you're involved in drugs at the degree I was, and hanging around the people at the bottom, it's survival of the fittest. A lot of people I knew did some pretty heinous things to support their habit. But I never got into that. That wasn't me. I didn't have to commit the crimes to survive in that world. The times I ran out of drug money, I wasn't about to go rob somebody, not even another drug addict, though there were plenty who tried to rob me. I was always able to use my name, my ability to negotiate my little hustle.

As soon as I got the money, I was back on crack. I was always welcome in crack houses. The other addicts liked seeing a guy like me, a guy who reached the top, now turned into such a loser. It made them feel better about themselves.

"Hey, look," they'd say. "It's 17-0."

I found out a lot about human nature during those years. The people driving the Mercedes-Benzes or Rolls-Royces usually would not help you. Maybe they saw through my hustle. Maybe they had money because they had never given it away. The people driving the mediocre cars, wearing the mediocre clothes, those were the ones who'd help you beyond the limits. They had a different view of life. A more grateful view.

Before I was driving around in broken cars with broken hoses—before I was broken down on drugs—I used to have my own Mercedes-Benz. It was a tan 450SL convertible with a chocolate canvas top and alloyed wheels. Before I was doing my little hustle, I had a good reputation, for good reason. I was trust-worthy. But before drugs, I had just one view of life—the view of a winner. Drugs showed me what it was like to be a loser in life. Nothing good came of my drug use. But it did make me humble again.

I'd quit drugs for a few months, cleaned up, but then dove back into that dangerous world. The entire time I was involved in drugs, though, I always knew I would get out for good someday. Get my life back. I had beaten the odds all my life. But overcoming drug addiction was my biggest obstacle yet.

2

Humble Beginnings

I was born September 10, 1945, in Oakland, California, to Marlin Briscoe and Geneva Moore. Not much is known about the breakup of my parents; nonetheless, they split when I was 4 years old. So my younger sister, Beverly—two years my junior—and I moved with my mother to Omaha, Nebraska, where we had relatives. Initially, we stayed with family members in North Omaha. We were close to the Kellom Center, a community center that had a pool, which was open to black residents of both South and North Omaha.

That was a significant building socially because it was the hub of the area for blacks. A lot of relationships were formed at that pool at a young age for black people. Young blacks would make friends—and perhaps adversaries—for life at that pool. Since none of the other Omaha pools allowed blacks, either implicitly or explicitly, that was our hangout in the summertime.

I often wondered even at a very young age why that was the only pool open to us? This was 1950, and in Omaha, Nebraska, it was hard for young African-American kids to understand why we were all pinned in one area in town. The same sort of segregation existed for housing; blacks were clustered in small areas of both South Omaha and North Omaha.

Being restricted to the one pool in summertime was my first real memory of racism.

Though it isn't the only memory of that nature.

I wondered: Why are things like this? Why do we have to stay in these particular areas? Why are we not welcome in other places? In fact, many immigrants coming to America were treated a lot better than blacks in most cities. Omaha was no exception.

The parks were the same way—we had certain parks that we could go to and others that we were not only unwelcome at, but were basically prohibited from visiting, even to just play on playgrounds.

After a year in North Omaha, my mother, who had come to Omaha to earn a living working in the meatpacking houses, decided she had enough income to afford a place for our small family. So we moved from North Omaha to the housing projects in South Omaha, closer to the packing houses. We lived on "S" Street, which was a relatively small project at that time. Of course, when you're a little kid, everything looks big, so I thought at the time that the projects were a much bigger complex than they really were.

My mother raised us in the black projects, which was a small part of the overall "projects"—which is to say that most in the projects were white. That was significant, though I did not understand why at the time. The blacks were clustered once again into one small area. I never understood that because everyone living in the projects had no money. Though there were no official boundaries, there were very real limits. We simply couldn't go in or near certain areas in the project or in the neighborhood. Walking to the store, I would pass through white areas. I would see white kids playing across the street from our project. But I couldn't go there.

I just didn't understand why. They played games just like we black kids did. They smiled and laughed like we did. My friends and I didn't get it. Perhaps that can be chalked up to the innocence of youth. We'd asked, "Hey, how come we can't play with those kids?" and point to whites. I didn't know the answer. It never dawned on us, at least at first that it was because of race.

When I did discover that it was just because of the color of our skin, it really bothered me.

We didn't have equality, but at home, in our family and our church we found sustenance. Though money was sparse, my mother always made sure my sister and I had everything we needed—love, shelter, food and clothes on our back. It wasn't fast food or delivered pizza three times a week. Clothes weren't GAP or Hilfiger. And home wasn't exactly the Hilton or a mansion. But, love was the important thing. And we had plenty of that. Since we had never had a lot of money, I didn't really understand the concept that we were poor—because I hadn't experienced any other lifestyle.

My mother is the most remarkable, resilient woman I've ever known in my lifetime. She was the "sage" of our neighborhood, very smart but very quiet. She was the treasurer for our church. And when I ended up going to Omaha University, my mother took a job in the cafeteria of the school, so she ended up being a mother to all the guys, black and white. She also got my close friend's mom a job at the cafeteria, Ulysses "Butch" Cribbs' mom. Butch was like a brother to me growing up.

My sister, Beverly, has always been a shiny gem in my life. My friends also liked her—sometimes more than I understood. In fact, I used to be baffled in high school about how my friends were always coming over to my house after school. I thought they were coming to see me, but it turned out that a lot of them had a crush on my sister, and I was their excuse to come over. Looking back, I think that's pretty neat, and it was a testimony to what a fine young woman that my sister was, and how well my mother raised her.

The projects were not a physically or aesthetically pleasing place. The first thing I remember noticing was the smell. Our particular project was located in the middle of a horseshoe formed by the meatpacking houses. The smell emanating from the packinghouses was putrid, especially at first. One really couldn't help but notice it. Only through time did we grow accustomed to the stench. The smell might have been bad, but it wasn't as bad as not having a place to live, not having food on the table or not even having second-hand clothes on your back. What were we to do about it, though? Nothing. That was where families earned a living.

The meatpacking houses also brought a service community of businesses to the surrounding area. The businesses spawned by the economic stimulus of the packinghouses were diverse. That brought people of various races and ethnic backgrounds to our area. We occasionally formed bonds with those people, though it was still mostly divided into black and white. In fact, I have neighbors that I lived beside for years and years whose names I never knew—never even met them, in fact. Yet there were people from North Omaha, a good drive across town, that I remained friends with for life.

As I grew older, I began to better understand the race issues. I became more informed as to why things were different among races, and every lesson was troubling. The saving grace for some in our neighborhood was that the packinghouses allowed some blacks to form bonds with other workers who were white. That too came with a cost, as the black and white workers were jockeying for higher-paying positions and promotions. If a white worker didn't get a promotion that went to a black, it could be made into a racial issue, just as it could if a white worker got a pay raise that a black wanted.

We had a park in our neighborhood, Upland Park. It was a nice, relatively clean inner city park, with playground equipment and lush green grass in the summer, and a few trees that looked good for climbing.

I never climbed those trees because the ladder of racism was missing several rungs at the bottom meaning blacks were excluded. Though that park was close to my home, I couldn't go there. I had to go to Kellom, where tensions would be high in the summer because of the intense heat and overcrowding. We had nowhere else to go, so we were packed in pretty tight. And going to Upland wasn't an option because simply setting foot there would mean a fight.

People in our units seven units in the black projects owned maybe two or three televisions. These weren't the days of 100-channel cable television. So we black kids would all pile into one apartment to watch TV. We'd rotate, going to different apartments on the weekends. We were a very close group "clan-like." We had our differences, certainly, but those friendships were for life. And race, while a dividing factor in the community, was something that brought us together in the projects.

As a kid, I used to watch sports on TV when I had the chance—football, basketball and baseball. I noticed there weren't any blacks on pro teams. There were a few blacks on college teams, but not many. I began to question why that was because it stuck in my mind as odd. We're all equal, I thought to myself, so why aren't any blacks playing pro sports? At that point, I didn't have an interest in playing football; I didn't think that sports would play such a prominent role in my future, so I probably put it more in the back of my mind.

That changed when I got more into sports, and when Jackie Robinson finally broke the color barrier. That spurred my interest in sports. While Jackie gained a lot of national and international attention, one of his biggest gifts was the one he gave to all of us black kids in the projects. He gave us hope. From the moment I saw his face and heard his name, I wanted to emulate Jackie Robinson and the few other black heroes I saw on TV competing in sports.

That black athletes weren't getting a fair chance was a reality of life. We blacks, even at an early age, were supposed to "have our place" and know that place. I knew several athletes who were very good. I looked up to them. I wondered why they didn't go to college. I would learn as I got into junior high and started high school that there weren't a lot of scholarships for black athletes. I didn't understand that. The odds were long and the opportunities few and far between. But watching my mother come home exhausted from her back-breaking, unrewarding, low-paying job helped me internalize something else: I knew I wasn't going to work in the meat-packing house my whole life. Sure, in order to make ends meet, or for spending money in high school, or to get through college, I might have to. But my whole life? Raising a family? That was not going to happen, no matter what.

In the 1950s—and in years to come—the packinghouses had a very significant impact on the shape of Omaha. A group of men made millions from the industry. "South O," as we call it, was a very unique neighborhood. There was no union. Although the wages were low, America wasn't yet two decades removed from the Great Depression, so the opportunity of gainful, plentiful employment was a blue ribbon for any community to pin on its civic shirt. Omaha had that ribbon because of the packinghouses. It brought a lot of immigrants from the coast. We had a very, very diverse community, so much so that we often called it the "Melting Pot" community, and in that regard it was quite different from North Omaha at the time. We certainly had our own ethnic flavor in South Omaha.

We had blacks and whites, of course, but a sizeable community of Hispanics as well. We also had the so-called refugees from the displaced countries in Europe, particular Poland and Germany. We had a very significant sized Asian community. All of these people came to find new freedoms and to work in the packinghouses. Until they found something better, the packinghouses gave them that opportunity. It was a community of people who knew little aside from the value of hard work. And that was enough to survive in this country, especially to those who lived in countries that had been torn up, physically and economically, by war.

Our community was also unique—at least to me—because it was a "family" as much it was a community. There was a lot of attention in the 1990s to the fact that "it takes a village" to raise a child. When I grew up, that was true. All of your neighbors took responsibility for helping raise you, especially in a case like mine where a single mother was raising two kids. In most cases, families were much bigger. It wasn't out of the ordinary to see a single mother raising five or six kids. The few fathers that were there were father figures to all of us. They made sure we had support. That helped our mothers with responsibility and accountability lessons for us. They looked after us, made sure we stayed out of trouble and gave us fatherly advice. Though I was most definitely raised by a single mother, I did have father figures, especially a cousin, Bob Rose, in my life.

We were a big family in that neighborhood. Though we didn't have a privacy fence securing our backyard, we were still kids, so we made due. We'd take blankets to the triangular patch of grass outside our apartment in the summer time and prop them up with sticks, making tents. The bats and the occasional stray dogs were all we had to worry about. We used to catch fireflies camping out there. This was a different era. That is, we never had to worry about someone coming along and bothering us. We did have drunks in the neighborhood, but none that bugged us. There weren't any drug addicts prowling around, no pedophiles. There was some alcoholism and spousal abuse, and some parents who beat their kids mercilessly. So it wasn't Mayberry on the Andy Griffith show. But by and large, it was a safe neighborhood with no guns and no real crime.

Though we were in apartments, a lot of the white kids from my school lived in houses. Some of their parents had a lot of education, which wasn't something blacks had the opportunity to do because of various circumstances and social attitudes. A lot of the black kids' parents had quit school before they graduated to work in the packinghouse. It wasn't until my generation, or perhaps the generation just before me, that blacks would pursue an education and not see the packing house as our/their future.

There were a lot of Air Force families in our neighborhood because Offutt Air Force Base was close by. Although the younger enlisted men did not make much money, the military families were very good, honest, hard-working people. Though I didn't support the war in Vietnam, I've always respected and supported the men and women who serve our country through the military. They were good neighbors, though they would be there for only a couple of years before moving. Still, it enabled us young kids to see another way of life with more diversity. That education was as important as any I would have ever gotten in any classroom. In that neighborhood, we had to co-exist with people of more diverse racial, social, cultural and ethnic backgrounds than I could ever list in entirety.

So looking back, I could not have asked for a better situation considering the predicament my mother faced as a single parent. I learned how to work and live with different people. That would suit me well, later in life.

When I was five, I started kindergarten in public school at Westside Elementary School. That was only five blocks from our apartment in the project. But as a kid, those five blocks seemed like miles. We would form into little groups, and the older kids would walk us younger kids to school, to make sure we got there without incident. Remember, for all of the healthy diversity in our neighborhood, there was constant, underlying racial tension there which was prone to ignite on a moment's notice and with a storm's fury.

The teachers at my school were all white, of course, as blacks weren't permitted (perhaps not always officially, but at least in practice) to teach in schools there were good people. We blacks were treated well. There was no racism that first year. Though there would be in the immediate years to come, I felt it was a good school, conducive to learning. I have to credit those teachers for being professional and caring. They saw something special in every child, regardless of race or ethnic background.

That gave me the best feeling a young boy can hope for; that is, I felt at a very young age that I had no limits on what I could do in life. In the 1950s, that was a great feeling for a young black to have because there weren't a lot of high profile, black leaders. Our history books failed at giving us black history or black leaders. Sure, we heard about Booker T. Washington and George Washington Carver, and nothing about anyone else. I would not learn until later in life that there were lots of black heroes.

I remember wondering, even as a 6-year-old first-grader, why black history was so limited. We talked a little about Little Black Sambo, which was a sore spot to me, because even at that young age, I realized something wasn't right with how blacks were portrayed.

Though in this day it would result in legal action, in those days you could be called a Little Black Sambo because it was part of the curriculum. I was very embarrassed to read about that in class. That was part of our studies, just as math and spelling were. That kind of thing and "Amos 'n' Andy" really stuck in my mind because the black people I knew were not like that. Sure, there were some characteristics that blacks seemed to have, but to portray those as a weakness, or as a lack of education and drive, bothered me deeply.

I went up to my first grade teacher after such a reading.

"Excuse me, why do have to read this kind of stuff?" I asked. "Black people are not all like that. Or the black people I know are not like that at all."

My teacher looked at me as though I was crazy. My guess is that my comment was relayed to other teachers because our teachers worked outside that kind of curriculum to make us feel like we could be doctors, lawyers or whatever we wanted—not just some stage act trying to make fun of how blacks spoke and walked different from whites.

I also felt like my teachers supported me in my interests. I listened and I asked questions. My teachers always answered and stimulated my interests. One of those was drawing, and I was pretty good. I liked singing in music class, and I really enjoyed PE and recess, especially playing ball. So those first two years of public school, I never heard any demeaning comments toward blacks. I was comfortable with the teachers, the school, and my place in it.

3

Encountering Racism

The first hurdle I had to stare down was in second grade. For the first time, I felt a limit—or at least a discriminatory (perhaps even blatantly racist) attitude. It was 1952, and I was in second grade at Westside. Every student had to take some form of music to, I'm sure, ensure we were well rounded and exposed to different forms of art and expression.

Each student had to play this black flute. Once we mastered the keys on the black flute, we'd graduate to the clarinet. I remember vividly when we were anxiously waiting to get the clarinets. There were two clarinets, one black and one brass colored. The black clarinets were better looking. I liked the clarinet and had an interest in it from watching Benny Goodman playing it on TV. I decided that I wanted to do that. So I was excited in music that we were headed that direction.

The teacher passed out the clarinets. The white kids got the nicer looking, more identifiable black clarinets. Then she moved to the black kids and gave them these ugly, brass clarinets. I received mine and frowned. So I got up immediately and went to her desk.

"I'd like a black clarinet, please," I said to my teacher.

She just looked at me. She thought I was obstinate, a troublemaker even, and sent me back to my seat. I didn't think I was being either, I simply wanted to get what I deserved, and I thought it was unfair that I didn't get a black clarinet.

"I just don't think that's fair," I said.

She was furious. That was the first incident that made me want to stand up for myself. How, I thought, could kids get the nicer instruments just because they were white? We were just kids.

My teacher didn't think that was the right attitude. She was so frustrated that she took me to our principal, Ida Gitlin, a white woman. She was from Greece, and she was a very stern woman. If she were a principal today, her school would not have a gang problem. On the one hand, she was as sweet and loving as a honeybun. But when someone wasn't acting right, she'd move swiftly, decisively, and very firmly, to fix the problems—always a no-nonsense approach. She would end up being one of the most influential people in my life.

No student wanted to be dragged to the principal's office, because they knew they wouldn't win. We feared "going to Mrs. G's office." She had a scowl when someone was out of line, and that brought you right back into line right away, in most cases.

As I found out that day, she had a very human and fair side to her. My teacher talked to her out of my earshot for a moment, and then Mrs. Gitlin came to me.

"What's going on Marlin?" she said, holding the brass clarinet. "What is wrong with this? Is it not good enough for you?"

I was almost shaking from her tone.

"Uh, well, it's good and all that," I stammered.

"Then," she said firmly, "what's the problem?"

"There is another one, a black clarinet, just like Benny Goodman's," I said.

"And you didn't get one of those," she said. "I don't see why that's a problem."

"It makes me mad because all of the white kids got the black ones, and if you're a black kid, you got this one—we all got the brass ones," I said.

Mrs. G turned her head, as if in thought. She excused me back to my class, which had returned to homeroom. She pulled aside the music teacher.

I went to school the next day, and had—as kids usually do—basically forgotten about the conflict, though I still wanted my black clarinet.

Well, what do you know! All of the kids had black clarinets, black kids, and white. Just like Benny Goodman's clarinet. As I look back, that was an important incident. I was able to learn at a young age that it wasn't just all right to stand up for yourself, but that it was the right thing to do. I could have backed down from my teacher and avoided the confrontation, much less being sent to the principal's office. But I didn't. And I didn't, even as a 7-year-old, view my actions as selfish. I didn't believe I had to settle for second best just because I was black. That really shaped me.

My school, looking back, was set in the right kind of neighborhood for me to grow. North Omaha—where we lived when we first moved to Nebraska—was predominantly black, at least in our neighborhood. So moving to South Omaha brought the challenge of interacting with a whole new (to me) set of people. Our neighborhood was small, so we had to come to grips with stereotypes pertaining both to blacks and white. We had to find out which if any of these stereotypes were really untrue. That was a difficult task on many occasions, from jockeying for position in class to playing sports on the playground. Kids are prone to use whatever they can to their advantage. If their parents have ingrained racial stereotypes into their kids—black or white—then those kids will use those when the time comes. So we had a lot of racial tension.

As black and white kids formed bonds, these stereotypes—and the accompanying tension—dissipated. Almost all of what we had heard about each other, from morality to intelligence, was dispelled as we became friends. You have to remember that many of our parents at that time were only three or four generations removed from slavery. So we had the blacks who correctly felt like they had been mistreated and were locked into a place in society. And we had whites who—though it had been their forefathers who owned slaves, not them—had an attitude of superiority for different reasons.

Compared to my neighborhood, school was a different world. How I wish it weren't, though.

Because at school, all the kids played together—white, black, European, Hispanic, you name it. When school ended, we would go home, and black kids would play with black kids, whites with whites, and so on. School gave us our only chance to interact. Take out all the social forces when kids are kids, they don't see color, only smiles. We were as smart as each other, as nice—or mean, in some cases—and we had the same interests and even maladies. It's just that our skin was different colors.

That opportunity to interact with other races and ethnic backgrounds was a big springboard for me. I honestly believe that the time with kids at school helped me learn how to work and even co-exist with people who were "different" from me.

Still, there came a time when I went to my mother, puzzled at how these huge barriers existed away from school, yet at school all the walls came down.

"Why can't I cross the street and play with Lupe Gomez (a Hispanic boy) or Jimmy Kearns (white)?" I asked my mother.

You have to understand; my mother was not racist. She never espoused a racist view, to me or to anyone I know. But that day she did honestly explain to me the views people had.

"Some white people think they're better than black people because of the color of their skin, and some blacks think they're better than white people for the same reason," my mother told me.

She explained that we were all the same inside. That we all smiled; we all cried, and when we bled, it was all red. We lived in the same neighborhoods. Our parents worked at the same jobs. We shopped at the same stores, for the most part. It didn't make sense to me. She explained to me very honestly what the real world was like. She told me about the separation of society, without injecting anger or prejudice. I marvel to this day at the beauty of my mother's heart and soul. The simple fact was—and is—this: Race is, at times, an issue.

I could turn on the TV and see it. And, really, I could even see it at school, such as the clarinet incident, and other cases. At times, we had fights between white and black kids at school, and these fists flew mainly because of race.

Thankfully, one day that barrier broke down for me after school. I was 8 years old, in the third grade. I made a new friend—one of the true everlasting beauties of school,—and his name was Jimmy Kearns.

I will never forget Jimmy.

He moved to Omaha from Chicago, so he was used to

befriending black kids. He was raised by his mother and had a brother and sister. Jimmy liked to comb his hair to look like Elvis. Black kids did that too because we all liked Elvis.

Jimmy and I formed a friendship and spent a lot of time together at school. I started walking home with him sometimes instead of with my black friends, usually when Jimmy and I stayed after school to shoot hoops. Boy, did we get flack from our friends for walking home together.

One day we were walking home, and Jimmy invited me over to his house. But he lived in THAT neighborhood, the one separated by 30 feet, though it was really a world away. My mother had always told me I couldn't go to that neighborhood because of the divisions set by race. So I told Jimmy, "I don't think I should."

Jimmy asked again a few days later, and I declined. The third time he asked me, as we were walking home, his mother was outside. I hesitated.

"Mom!" Jimmy called out. "Can Marlin come over and play?"

"Sure!" his mother yelled and waved. "Come on in!"

So I did. We had a great time, and I met his family. A couple of days later, we were walking home, and I asked him to come over. He did. My mother wasn't there. She was surprised—but not at all angry—when she came home and met Jimmy. She liked him, and Jimmy thought my mom was great. But she pulled me aside that night after he went home.

"Marlin, don't be disappointed if the friendship doesn't last," she told me. "At some point, the friendship could end because of how people are."

My mother was a very wise person. She'd do hair and play the piano. She always told me about life, explained things to me. Because of her position in the church and in the social circles, people were always at our doorsteps. She helped us make a lot of friends. My mother was a pivotal person in my development, and my sister's development—and even for a lot of the other young kids in my neighborhood. A lot of kids came to her for advice. This was a very tumultuous time in how America treated its black citizens, both young and old. She was only looking out for me.

But the friendship with Jimmy grew. He became friends with some of my black friends, and I became friends with some of his white friends. Jimmy Kearns was the first white friend I ever had, and he was a great friend. I remember when his skin got cut; he bled red, just like me—just like my mother had told me.

Our friendship was hard—on both of us—at times. It was like a constant standoff. We blacks couldn't go past 36th Street, though it was only six blocks away, because it wasn't considered "our territory." Going there meant there was a chance of getting into fights. After word got out that I had gone to Jimmy's house, he got into fights with white kids who didn't like him hanging out with a black kid. But he'd stand up for himself and not back down. Eventually, they left him alone. First of all, Jimmy could fight. Secondly, he was just making friends—he wasn't trying to be black or white. That gesture on his part softened the culture in our little corner of the world.

Other black and white kids became friends. It wasn't easy, and it led to fights, but for the most part we moved past that. And it was great to see white kids in our neighborhood. You see, when you're young, you're kind of naïve about life; you get hurt when you face down prejudice—whether you're facing down on purpose or not. But those are learning experiences. And it shapes you as a person.

We couldn't go to a lot of the recreation centers in South Omaha. We did have one by the projects called the Woodson Center. That place was probably the most important place in all of South Omaha outside of the church. It was a safe haven after school. Alice Wilson, who was black, ran the center. She was a no-nonsense person who had a lot of love. Anyone who came through the door to the center was welcome. There were a few ladies who worked there, Mrs. Mosley and Mrs. Thomas, who really looked out for us and made us be responsible. We weren't allowed to play ball until our homework was done each day. We had to show them our completed assignments before we could get a ball.

They also offered classes on everything from cooking to sewing. And they had a library. They divided our days into half-hour segments. You did the classes and homework, and then you could go to the library. If you completed everything, you could play in the gym for the last segment. That was an important training ground for black kids, and it was the hub of our neighborhood for blacks.

Closer to my home was another center, but it was in the "white settlement" so we couldn't use their gym—and they couldn't come to ours. That was a constant reminder of the "differences" among us.

Fighting was a way to deal with problems and conflicts when I was a kid. Not that it was the right way, but it was the way in a lot of cases. Me, personally? I didn't like to fight, even though I had agility and ability in sports, which probably means I could hold my own. Though the guys in the neighborhood were like big brothers and their fathers were surrogate fathers to me, I never really had a dad to wrestle around with and teach me to "be brave" and stand up for myself when confronted with a "fight or flight" situation.

Sometimes, I'd flat run away. I'd get called yellow. It wasn't that I was scared. I just didn't want to fight. I had several confrontations where I'd run home to get out of it. But at that age—I was 8 years old—kids can be cruel. If you didn't stand up and fight, you were labeled a coward. As I said, growing up without a father, I didn't have someone to teach me how to defend myself. I suppose I knew how to, but it was the mental part—and the plain truth is that I wanted to get along with everyone.

But there comes a point where you have to stand up for yourself.

There was a neighbor boy who would bully me. He'd dare me to fight.

"Cross over this line," he said.

"I don't want to fight," I answered.

He picked up a rock and set it on his shoulder.

"Knock this rock off my shoulder," he baited.

"I don't want to," I said.

It started off with me walking away. Then, it escalated to him chasing me all the way home. One of those days, my mother was home. She saw me panting, short of breath, as I got in the door and hurriedly slammed it shut behind me.

"Marlin, would you like to tell me what's going on?" she asked.

"This kid," I gasped, "chased me home, again."

"Again? What do you mean, again?" she asked. "This has been going on a while, has it? Sit down."

I explained what was going on to her.

"I don't want you to fight, you know that," she said, putting her hand on my shoulder. "But this is worse."

"But, Mom, I don't fight," I said.

"This, Marlin, is worse," she said. "He can't oppress you. He can't control you. He can't decide where you go and make you run home each day."

"I just want to get along with everyone," I said.

"Marlin, in the real world, it doesn't always work that way," she said.

She didn't like that I was whining and not standing up for myself.

"Defending yourself isn't the same thing as going around picking fights," my mother said.

Curiously enough the next day, my cousin, coach Bob Rose, came by the house. Being my all-time hero, Bob always had my undivided attention. He had attended Boys Town and starred on the football and basketball team. He played single wing (a run-oriented form of offense) quarterback at Omaha University, and played on the college basketball team. Bob was my idol. He wasn't allowed—be it practically or pragmatically—to coach in Omaha high schools because he was black. But he was the best coach Omaha ever produced. He coached so many of us who would make it to the pros. It appalls me that he never got to realize his dream of coaching at a high school.

At the time, Bob was teaching and coaching in an elementary school in North Omaha, where black teachers were allowed. This was summer, and he was working in the packinghouse to make ends meet.

My mother wasn't home from work yet.

"Hi, Marlin, it's good to see you," he said, smiling. "But I'm here because there's a problem."

I felt a twinge. I thought about it: Had I done anything wrong? No. I wasn't in trouble at school. And I hadn't been in trouble at home.

WHAM!

Bob thumped me upside the head, square in the temple. It was all I could do to keep from falling as I staggered to keep my balance. He was not a huge man, 6-foot, 175 pounds, but he was strong and in great shape.

"Your mother told me some kid bullied you, and you ran away," Bob said. "What's up with you, Sad Sack?"

That hurt worse than the smack—being called Sad Sack. I had heard Bob call kids he coached that name when they under-achieved and he was upset. Now, I was Sad Sack. I saw the anger in his eyes, but I also saw the love. The kid bullying me had scared me, but that had, in turn, hurt Bob Rose.

"So you run away and don't stand up for yourself?" Bob asked rhetorically. "You're being a coward?"

"Thanks, Mom," I whispered under my breath, in disbelief my mom had told Bob what I had divulged to her the previous day.

"What's that, Marlin?" he shot back.

I looked at the ground. I was ashamed mostly that Bob was dis-appointed in me. I never wanted to disappoint my hero. I felt like crying, but I didn't; I wasn't going to disappoint Bob anymore than I already had. He could see the pain I felt, my lip quivering, trying to stand as upright as possible, offering this general the best little soldier look I could muster.

"Hey, it's gonna be all right," he said, patting me on the head—gently this time. "Tomorrow, I'm coming over after work, and we're going to straighten this out. Problem's over tomorrow, bud. I'm going to bring you something. I never want to hear from your mother again about how you're not defending yourself."

"Yes, sir," I said. He pushed up my chin, looking into my eyes.

"Marlin, it's all going to be all right, I can tell you that much," Bob said, and I could see the love in his face, hear the care in his voice. "We're going to take care of things. A lot of things. You up for that?"

"Yes, sir," I said.

He patted me on the shoulder, playfully picked me up and then headed to the door.

The next day, I couldn't imagine what cousin Bob had in store for me. Maybe he'd come and beat up the bully! That would be great! But that wouldn't solve the problem. And Bob Rose, the great athlete and coach, didn't go around beating up kids—unless it was his cousin who wouldn't defend himself. Maybe he'd tell another of the older kids to take care of the bully? Well, I certainly thought that was a great idea, but it wouldn't really solve the problem of me not defending myself. And that was the problem Bob wanted to solve—he wanted me to stand up for myself, not someone else to stand up for me.

The next day, I waited at home for Bob. Sure enough, not 15 minutes after his shift ended at the packing center, he was walking up the sidewalk toward our apartment. He had this big box that read "Howard Kennedy School" on the side of it.

The "magic box."

4

The "Magic Box"

Inside the box were all kinds of sports equipment and balls for all kinds of sports. They were all far from new—closer, in fact, to being headed for the scrap heap, and the dust on them made them appear that much more worn. Bob couldn't bring me new equipment, though. I surely understood that.

I will never forget that day. It remains vivid in my mind as though I can reach out and grab the football or basketball right now. Bob was about to take me down a road that would change the direction of my life—my entire life, from a young boy to a man. Looking back I was at a very impressionable age. Bob stepped in at the exact right moment. I was about to head in the right direction.

We went out to that triangle-shaped patch of grass that was a front yard for six other families and us. It was maybe 50 feet to the street. So it wasn't large, but it was a place for us kids, who didn't have a white picket fence, to play.

Bob pulled out this old baseball and glove. He showed me how to throw, catch and even hit a baseball. I remember the web was almost gone in the glove, so I became very efficient at catching fundamentally correct, with both hands. He showed me the proper way to swing a bat.

"No, no, keep your elbow up," he instructed me as I swung wildly. "You want to be under control and make contact with the ball. It doesn't matter how hard you can swing. You can swing as hard as you want, but if you don't make contact with the ball, it isn't going anywhere."

We played baseball catch and he taught me how to hit until it was dark.

Each day we played another sport—soccer, basketball (we used the soccer ball for that), you name it. He would look at me each day, and he could see I had athletic ability—that I picked things up rather quickly. Mind you, he never said that, but it was clear in his eyes that he could see it.

A few days later, we got to football. He admitted that he was surprised I could throw and catch, and that I had good form. I said that I wanted to be a quarterback. In those days, blacks weren't quarterbacks because they weren't taught the fundamentals. Those lessons were for white kids. It was believed blacks couldn't pass, but it was only because we were never taught the technique. It was all technique. Black kids weren't coached to play quarterback. So for two weeks, day after day, we worked on all the sports.

There was a set of boxing gloves in that magic box. Bob taught me to jab and punch so I could protect myself. That set the tone for the confidence I needed to survive in my environment.

On what turned out to be the final day of my "sports boot camp" he thumped me upside the head again.

"What's that for?" I said, rubbing my temple.

"I gave those thumps to guys like Gale Sayers and other guys you'll hear about some day, because they're going to be great athletes and responsible adults," Bob said. "And they're not going to run away from bullies, either. You got that?"

Though it would be years down the road, Gale Sayers went on to become a legend. Johnny Rodgers, several years younger than me, won the Heisman Trophy at Nebraska. Bob saw their talent. He was a great coach and purveyor of talent. Bob left that day, but what he taught me never left. Indeed, it only grew. Bob never told me I had to go out and practice. But I did, every day. I never did pursue baseball or soccer seriously—though I had ability and aptitude for baseball—but I did work hard at football and basketball. My confidence was soaring. I took the soccer ball and shot baskets. I loved to practice. I had the right technique, so my improvement was more than gradual. Things came quickly to me.

I finally ran into the bully again a week later when school had started. He approached me on the way home from school, obvi-

ously sure that I'd back down and take off running. He kept pushing me.

"I don't want to fight," I kept saying over and over.

He pushed again. And again. Pretty soon, something inside me
reminded me of the thump Bob had given me. I knew another one
was coming if I didn't stand up for myself. And nothing that bully
could do would hurt more than one of Bob's thumps to the temple.
This wasn't the day of knives and guns. This was an era of fists,
earning respect by standing up for yourself. And it was time I did
just that.

So we fought. Much to my amazement, this fight didn't end up
with me either running or on the ground. I'd say that I won that
fight. That bully realized that if we kept going at it, I'd be the one
chasing him home. That led to respect, and ironically, it led to a
great friendship with the kid.

My self-confidence was hitting new levels. The discipline of
practice extended to school. I was more confident in expressing
myself. I knew kids who excelled in sports got more of the good
attention from teachers and peers alike. That happened to me, all
because of what Bob Rose taught me. My grades soared.

I became obsessed with the "magic box." I couldn't wait to get
home to the small patch of grass and practice. I would go from one
sport to another, more often than not alone, just in my own little
world. I really didn't need any playmates, which was good, because
there weren't many around. So I'd play with my invisible teammates—a tree as if I were throwing the baseball. I'd shoot baskets
at an imaginary basket on the wall, playing against Bob Cousy.
When I was about 11 or 12, I'd be Johnny Unitas, throwing to a tree
that in my mind was the great receiver Raymond Berry. Through
that magic box, I uncovered a new world. That box was my play-
mate, my best friend. It brought me confidence. In PE and recess at
school, my improvement was noticeable. My dexterity and agility
were improving by leaps and bounds. My teachers and classmates
were noticing. I thrived on their encouragement and got better and
better.

Bob was very self-assured, very confident, and very tough. He
was a no-nonsense kind of guy, which was what young kids needed at that stage of their lives. He came into our lives when we all
could have gone one way or another. Gale Sayers was a semi-hood-

lum when Bob took him under his wing. Bob coached Gale in midget football and in junior high football.

Bob was an amazing coach and mentor. It's a shame he was never allowed to prove his mettle as a high school coach. I wonder what Omaha high school sports could have become if he were allowed to show his worth as a teacher, coach and human being. Kids would have reached new levels of achievement on the field of competition and in the classroom. Young boys would have become more responsible men.

Soon thereafter, I was baptized at Bethel Baptist Church as a 9-year-old, in 1954. The church was also instrumental in forming my values and a lot of my goals. In those days, the church was the informational hub of the community especially for blacks, not only for religion, but life. So that year was a turning point in my life.

At the Woodson Center, I soon became one of the better athletes. We didn't have organized sports there, but we did play basketball, volleyball—even dodgeball. We'd box and wrestle. I just seemed to excel. Bob and the magic box uncovered and sculpted what would develop into a lifetime pursuit of goals, many of which were athletic. It also stimulated me intellectually, from the discipline and commitment that grew out of that box of dusty sports equipment.

Watching sports on TV became more than just entertainment. It became a part of me. Watching Unitas really got me going. The vision is still clear in my mind of Unitas in those high-top shoes with the command and respect he had from all of his teammates. Still, I was curious why no blacks were playing quarterback, or playing in any professional sport. But the few I did see playing pro sports helped fuel that fire in me. Maybe it IS possible, I thought.

My mother and neighbors would watch from the windows as I ran through my drills out front, throwing that football in the rain and snow. When I first started, I was lucky to hit the tree once out of 10 tries. Not long thereafter, I'd be disappointed if I didn't hit it every time, scrambling out of the way as imaginary defenders chased me, forcing me to throw at the tree while running the other way, or throwing off my back foot.

The older kids in the neighborhood saw me, and allowed me to play in their pick-up games, first of flag football and then tackle football. None of the other kids in the neighborhood had been taught to throw, in terms of the mechanics, technique and footwork. So even though I was one of the younger kids playing, the older kids let me play quarterback—and I was the smallest kid out there. I'd call plays. I began to covet the position of quarterback.

I had a good circle of close friends from a very young age. Ronnie Kellogg and Eddie Hayes, who was my next-door neighbor, were part of that circle, though both were several years older than I was. They saw something in me, and took me under their considerable wings. Eddie was a musician, a very good one, but not much of an athlete. Ronnie was probably one of the best athletes who never made it to college. He could do it all. He was a good-looking guy who had a lot of girls chasing him around. He knew the mechanics of throwing the football and he worked with me. It was through Ronnie that I learned about Pop Warner football.

There was a team in our area sponsored by Philips Department Store, which at that time was a fixture in South Omaha. There was a tough hurdle to clear, though; my mother didn't want her child playing football, thinking I'd get hurt. After a lot of pestering, she let me sign up. She consulted my cousin, Coach Bob Rose, who was elated that I had made the decision.

Bob took me to the courthouse where I was weighed and had to show a birth certificate to prove I was old enough. I saw a bunch of kids I'd never met before, though we were all pretty much from the same neighborhood. Bob got me registered. I was very, very nervous the first day of tryouts. As kids are prone to do, we sized each other up, sometimes staring down, other times avoiding eye contract. My blood was pumping.

The tryouts were at a place named Christie Heights Park, about three-quarters of a mile from my house. That was also an area that was "off-limits" to black kids. I went with a friend of mine, Robbie Walls, a black kid. There were only three of us blacks at the tryout in the "white" park.

The coach appeared to be white—and black. His name was Simon A. Simon, Jr., a man of Greek descent, who would later play lineman for a semi-pro team, the Omaha Mustangs. His father, Simon A. Simon, Sr., was a judge in Omaha.

Simon Jr.—Coach Simon—was smart, very community minded and a good athlete. He took time out to coach little league football and give something back to the community. In him, I saw a fair and open-minded person, which I knew I needed.

Because what was going to happen next would require someone who could handle it. He was about to see a black quarterback in that white park. And it didn't take a month of research to know there hadn't been a black kid playing quarterback there before.

Coach Simon did the standard pep talk, explaining the league, the philosophy and rules. Then, he divided us into groups and told kids to go to the position they wanted to play. Of course, he and the other coaches didn't know the particular players' talents and personal goals at that point, and certainly kids would shift to other positions as it became apparent their talents were more suited for another position or less suited, as it were.

"Offense, over here!" Coach Simon yelled in his powerful voice. "Defense, over there!"

A group of us hustled over to where the offense was to form.

"Quarterback line, over here!" Coach Simon called out. "Defensive back line, over there! Linebacker, here! Everybody understand?"

"Yes, sir!" we answered.

He went on, calling out all the positions, and lines formed as everybody went to the line of their choice. I, of course, went to the quarterback line.

"Son," Simon said, "don't you think you're in the wrong line?"

"No, sir," I said, looking him in the eye.

"This is the quarterback line," Coach Simon said, looking at me and sizing me up. "Why don't you go over to the running back line, or you can even play defense?"

To be honest, I had some baby fat, I was kind of pudgy in those days, so Coach Simon said, "Hey, look, you could even play on the line."

"Coach," I said, "I'd like to play quarterback."

I saw a fair man. I saw honest eyes as he looked at me, pursed his lips together in a sort of acknowledgement if not an outright smile, and said, "OK, let's get practice started."

We did calisthenics and then did handoff drills. I was always the best one, but I was always put to the back of the line, not just because of my color, but because they had kids who had played quarterback the year before. So I didn't view being at the back of the line as a social injustice or anything.

I completed all the handoff drills. My footwork was solid. The last drill was the passing drill. The theory across the country, from Pop Warner football to college and pro football, was that black football players couldn't throw with proper mechanics, or even throw a spiral. We lined up to do short-range and long-range passes.

To say I was nervous would be a huge understatement. But I remember watching Johnny Unitas and how he said to always be "cool under fire." So whatever butterflies I had would have to take a backseat because I needed to be cool under fire.

The other quarterbacks went first, and coaches watched for accuracy and what kind of touch the pass had.

Finally, it was my turn.

A lot of people were watching me, including some black friends who showed up at the white park to make sure I got a fair chance.

I remember the day as if it were yesterday—or even this morning. Coach Simon might not have been truly shocked to see a black in the quarterback line, though I was told he had never had a black tryout for quarterback before. Like I said, I was kind of chubby. So here I am, this roly-poly kid who couldn't afford spikes—I had oversized shoes that I had cut with a knife to make them look like low-cut spikes—cleats weren't given out unless you made the team.

So much went through my mind before my first pass.

I remember what Ronnie and Eddie had told me in terms of what to do: be calm and make sure I do as well as I could with every opportunity. The one thing they did tell me was that I would not get as many repetitions or opportunities to throw as the other quarterbacks. This had a lot to do with the perception that blacks could not play quarterback. So I learned that at a very early age.

I also knew that Coach Simon had a good reputation and that he was not a racist. But honestly, he was probably naïve and uneducated in regard to a black being quarterback Coach Simon, as I would learn, was very fair. If not for Coach Simon, I would never have had that first chance to play quarterback.

We started the drills, and I succeeded in the short-range throws, making handoffs and pitching the ball. I made sure I did the tosses the right way—with both hands. I raised eyebrows and got a few smiles.

When I threw the long-range passes, eyebrows were raised like McDonald's Arches.

"Son," a smiling Coach Simon said afterward, "you did a great job today. You can play quarterback."

Those words tickled me. I was on Cloud Nine. But I didn't want to show it. I stayed calm on the outside, but inside, my heart was pumping. I couldn't wait to get home and tell my neighborhood what had happened because they were behind me. My friends knew, even at that early point in time, that football could be disappointing for me.

I ran to the Woodson Center on the way home and told everyone how well I did. They were surprised—but not surprised that I had done well. They were surprised that I got the opportunity.

The next day, all of my neighbors who hadn't come that first day came to practice just to make sure that I got a fair shake and an opportunity to show what I could do. I don't know if Coach Simon was uneasy with all of my neighbors being there. That provided a bittersweet feeling because on the one hand, I wanted to do it on my own. On the other hand, it meant a lot that my neighbors rallied behind me because they wanted to see this little black kid get a chance to play quarterback. It also made me nervous because I had to perform, so the added pressure was there. We all walked home together that day. They agreed that if there were ever an opportunity for a black to play quarterback in midget football, Coach Simon would be the one to provide that chance.

I made the team that year, but I didn't play quarterback. I was the third-team quarterback, and only the top two got to play. I started at defensive back. That gave me confidence. And being the "emergency quarterback" gave me confidence that I could be the quarterback the next year, which I did.

My first year in organized football was a learning experience. I played mostly defense. We played our first game of the season at Boys Town against Roberts Dairy. They had running backs by the name of Gale Sayers and his brother Roger Sayers. Gale was as great then as he would be in his collegiate and professional career.

Gale was bigger than a lot of us. I will never forget a play in that game. Gale broke through the line and I was the only one to stop him. Instead of Gale running around me, he ran right through me, just stomped over me and into the end zone. I remember crying, not because he had hurt me, but because he wounded my pride; I was the only one who could stop him, and I didn't. I vowed that wouldn't happen again. Of course, it would happen again, but I gained a lot of determination to become a better player.

As I mentioned, Bob had coached Gale and all the great athletes from the Midwest in that era. The kids came through and learned from Bob during those critical years of development in an athlete's career. I don't think Gale—or a lot of others—would have reached their potential without Bob. Not only from a talent or athletic standpoint but also from the discipline.

When I did get the chance at age 11 to play quarterback, the incumbent quarterback was Donnie Crum. His brother Denny was one of my very best friends from grade school. Donnie was a year older than me and a great athlete in his own right in all sports. Ironically, I would follow in his footsteps all the way through high school.

Since Donnie was a year ahead of me, I would always replace him on the team, from grade school through junior high and high school. I became friends with Donnie and Denny, who were both white. Donnie could hold his own with anybody. He was a tough kid on and off the field. He was never afraid. And his brother and I were very close. Denny has since died. But I was a fixture in their family home; we visited each other's homes and became close.

So when I got a chance to play quarterback, I was excited. I did have to share the job, though, with Joe Berenis, a good friend, who was white. We had twins who were good receivers and overall athletes, Lon and Ron Bernth, who would go on to baseball careers at Omaha University.

Joe was a good basketball player and quarterback. We were the ones last in line during that practice when I got my first shot at quarterback. So all through midget football, flag football and high school, Joe and I were co-quarterbacks for our team, splitting playing time. We learned the position together, and I think we both benefited from that. We remain friends to this day.

I also played basketball, something I love as much as football. When football season was over, basketball quickly took its place. I found that, especially when I was younger, I was a better basketball player than football player was. I played a lot of basketball during the winters at the Woodson Center.

After lunch at elementary school, I'd sneak away and go to the gym. That always made me late for class. One day the teacher, Mr. McMahan, came looking for me. He heard the ball bouncing in the little gym, which was nothing more than a cracker box. There I was, with a volleyball, shooting and dribbling against make-believe players. That teacher was also a coach for the junior high basketball team. He did chastise me—as was his duty—for being late for class. But he kept me after class and talked to me. I told him I liked sports.

"You have to get to class on time and do your school work first," he told me. "You can't be late from shooting hoops. But come by and see me when school's out, and we'll practice basketball every day for 15 minutes, if you'd like."

Like it? I loved it. I guess he saw something in me at that point. The way he dealt with me was important. Yes, he was hard on me because I had to make that commitment to schoolwork. But he did it in such a way that he encouraged me to pursue sports, yet only under the right conditions. I believe that was an important factor in my life, to have people like that—educators and mentors—from outside of my neighborhood who gave me a lot of support and believed in my ability at a young age.

I spent a lot of time in the gym and got better and better as the school year ended. The good instruction really drove up my level of play, especially the fundamentals. One day a few weeks later, my cousin, Coach Bob Rose, came over to the house.

Bob was always "Mr. Rose"—to everyone. He coached all sports in North Omaha. When he came by that day, he said he needed another player for his summer basketball league, which started play that weekend. I was to take the place of a kid named Jody Sinclair.

"So you want to play?" Bob asked.

"Of course!" I beamed.

"There is one catch," Bob said. "Jody's name is already on our roster. So you will have to play using his name."

I was young, so I didn't know if that was right or wrong. All I knew is that I wanted to play. He took me over to the gym at Howard Kennedy School and introduced me to the players, who had never seen me play. Later on, I would become life-long friends with those kids.

However, at that first practice, the players didn't know what to make of me. They knew I was Bob's cousin, so they thought I'd be the Coach's pet. They quickly saw how hard I'd play in practice, so that dispelled any myths.

On a more practical level, the first thing I had to do was learn how to spell Jody's last name—Sinclair—correctly, no small feat considering it was a unique name and that I'd be under pressure. If I signed in wrong, it would get the team, the Coach, and me in trouble. We went to the tourney in Omaha, and I passed the first test, signing Sinclair's name correctly. The older players ribbed me about that because it showed signs of intelligence and common sense. I made a good friend on that team, a kid named Johnny Alexander, who was a guard. Our paths and addictions, though different, would cross again decades later in Los Angeles. Johnny was a good player, and he helped me fit in on the team right away.

I wasn't a starter for the first game. The format was a three-day, single-elimination tournament. We got behind in the first game, so I started playing like I did when my teacher had been coaching me in the cracker box gym at school. I scored a few points and we won the game. So for the next game, Bob had no problem putting me in the game—I even started. By then, the kids were excited to have me on the team. There were no perceptions of nepotism. We won the second game, so we were to play in the final.

We were the underdogs even though we had a pretty good team. The other team had a guy named Bob Becker, 12 years old, and clearly one of the best players in the age group. We ended up beating his team 25-21, and I had 15 points. It was great. The tournament was so big that it even got some newspaper coverage. There it was in the paper that we won, "led by Jody Sinclair's 15 points, and Sinclair shared Co-Most Valuable Player honors with Benson's Bob Becker."

Though it wasn't the ideal circumstance, it was a valuable lesson. I had to deal with anonymity after starring in the spotlight. I wouldn't get lauded or applauded for my ability. I did get the pat on the back and respect of my team. Ironically, that meant the most, far more than a public pat on the back. In life, we don't always get credit for the good things we do. And if you are in a position where you do something good, you should never, ever have to point it out to anyone. You will get what you deserve. And I did. It also brought home the importance of "team" to me. Winning as a team is more important than any one player's agenda. I know the 15 points wouldn't have meant much to me if we lost. It was that first-place trophy that holds the best memory. I never told anyone, "That was me!"

People ended up seeing the paper and asking Jody how it felt to win MVP. He told people it was Marlin Briscoe, so in my own little circle I ended up getting more congratulations. That whole experience ingrained in me the importance of humility and the need to balance ego with the real purpose of winning and helping the team. Yes, I now know, it was illegal. But it happened. And it helped me grow as a person. Athletes always want to see their name in lights. But handling adulation and disappointment are also important, and that experience did both for me.

Between eight and nine, I began to look at life as more of a teen than a third or fourth grader. Give kudos to my teachers and the physical education teachers in elementary school because they nurtured those grandiose horizons that existed in my young mind. For some reason those educators saw something in me and were willing to make me believe that I could challenge the stereotypes and do what I wanted to in sports.

In Junior High, I ended up playing against a team Bob coached. I was the starting quarterback for our eighth-grade flag football team. Bob coached Howard Kennedy from across town. We played them for the city championship. Here I was playing against the man who taught me everything I knew. Our team was a real underdog, and I don't think anyone really thought we had a chance because Bob's teams were always so good, especially this particular year.

Several of my teammates from midget football were on Bob's team. We played a real back and forth, hard fought battle. We ended up winning a close game. Bob, being very competitive, was very disappointed afterward. I saw him across the field when time ran out. He consoled his players and our eyes met. He winked at me and mouthed, "Good job." I could tell he was proud of me. He came over to the house that day and told my mother how well I had played.

Bob did get me back in the city basketball championship. I had a great game, but it wasn't enough. Bob's team won. Still, I was happy that I played well and that my team had made it to the final. Bob was the big brother and father I never had. He will always hold a special place in my heart.

As high school loomed on the horizon after my ninth grade year, I had a decision to make—which high school to attend. Living in South Omaha, all of the kids coming out of the projects dreamed of going to South High and following all of the great athletes and scholars who had attended South through the years. It was, and is, a storied high school with great, rich tradition.

I had great allegiance and pride to what South had done, following them through all the years growing up and going to their sports games. But I was torn because a guy I considered to be like a brother—Ulysses Cribbs, whom I would see experience the highest of highs and ultimate lows in years to come—was going to Omaha Central High School. And I could go there if I wanted to. Ultimately, I chose South. Ulysses and I stayed very close, though, and would cross paths again, first in college, and then in a nightmare of a scene in an Omaha courtroom, in years to come.

As a sophomore at South, Joe Berenis and I again split the quarterback duties. When Joe was quarterbacking, I played halfback. One of South's trademark plays was the halfback pass, and that worked well with me in the game, so we used it often.

As a junior, Joe and I again split time at quarterback, and I was halfback.

5

Breaking a Barrier

Also during my junior year of high school, I was elected to the student council. Again, I had no idea that it was a big deal. But it turned out I was the first black to serve in such a position. I learned about protocol and how to hold meetings—diplomacy, all those kinds of things. Since there were only seven blacks in my class of 550, I realized it was an honor to be selected to the student council by my peers. It wasn't because I was a jock, though I was captain of the football and basketball teams. I wanted to be a leader outside of sports. I had good grades and was the consummate student, so being involved in student issues was a logical extension of making high school the well rounded experience that it should be.

My senior year, I was elected president of the student council. That was another honor. The previous year, the president was Pauline Williams, a very, nice intelligent person who would later be inducted to the South High School Hall of Fame with me.

As student council president, I had to be a diplomat with all students, and I had a lot of interaction with the teachers and the administration. At the senior prom, South High had a tradition that had the president of the senior class dancing with the president of the student council if they were of different genders. Such was the case that year with the Class of 1963. The senior class president was Anne Hoffman, a good friend of mine then, and today, as is her husband, Bill Allen.

Anne was a salt of the earth kind of person, very intelligent, witty and well spoken. But, before the Senior Prom, the student government counselor came to me and said that Anne and I wouldn't be dancing since I was black and she was white, and that, I was told, made the thought of carrying on the tradition of dancing together a real taboo. I didn't want to make waves, so I just nodded. I told Anne, and she was livid.

"No way. That is completely wrong," Anne said. "Marlin, we will dance."

Back in those days, the kids didn't grow up with racist views. We were taught those by adults who modeled such behavior. We were naive, even innocent, if you will. The racism was a product of the environment created by adults. Anne said we would dance, and I agreed. So we danced, and all the kids just loved it. I never viewed it as thumbing my nose at the school or the counselor. Rather, it was doing the right thing, carrying on a school tradition, but more importantly breaking down the racial barriers that those who came before us had erected.

Racism, I felt, was also threatening to keep me from a college sports scholarship. Though my high school career had been successful, I started to realize that I might not get an opportunity to get to college on a scholarship. I had to plan out my own way to make it work, which might mean paying my own way.

As a senior in football, I played only running back. I didn't play quarterback at all. Joe quarterbacked, and our team was very good, earning a share of the city championship. The people in my neighborhood cried racism as the reason I didn't get to play quarterback. I wanted to be a team player and fit in, so I just did what the coaches said. I was chosen all-city at running back.

Every day I checked the mail hoping a scholarship offer would come through. Aside from some very small schools, there were no takers. Needless to say, I was very disappointed, and somewhat surprised because my statistics, talent and work ethic seemed to me, and a lot of people, to be more than enough to compete at the Division I level in college.

Like all Nebraska school boys who ever picked up a football— and even many who did not—my dream was to play for the University of Nebraska, which was an hour away in Lincoln. Every schoolboy wanted to don the helmet with the "N" and play for the Big Red.

Some of the athletes against whom I competed—and had done better than—were getting scholarships to Division I colleges. I couldn't believe it. What was holding me back? Surely, it was a coincidence that it was mostly white kids getting scholarships, or at least I hoped that was the case. Since I was 5-foot-10, I realized my size might be an issue. Still, I really believed I'd get an opportunity.

Eventually, I had to swallow the bitter pill of racism and politics as the situation unfolded. Another young black male was going to be allowed to fall through the so-called cracks, it seemed.

I wasn't going to let that happen.

And the forum that presented itself was very odd. Once again, the script unfolded in a way that was very unpredictable. Every year, Nebraska has a state all-star contest, called the Shrine Bowl, which features the best players from across the state.

I was selected to the South team. The quarterback for the North team was Bob Churchich, who went to North High School. Churchich was a high-school all-American. Churchich, along with South quarterback Wayne Weber, was headed to the University of Nebraska on scholarship. Weber would go on to back up Churchich for the Huskers throughout the pair's career in Lincoln.

I was to back up Weber on the South team at quarterback—though I played running back in high school, another irony that would keep my budding college dreams plugging along through a difficult time of being overlooked by colleges.

The coaches for the South Shrine team must've been the fairest in the land.

They had 6-foot-3 Wayne Weber, Nebraska recruit who was a good friend of mine. Surely, he would be the starter, or so everyone thought heading into practices for the South team.

When Wayne was injuried, I received the starting nod. I simply fared better in the drills and running the plays in practice for the Shrine Bowl. I threw the ball well the entire week of practice after not playing quarterback in more than a year. That raised a lot of eyebrows at the University of Nebraska, I am sure. And it was an exciting moment for me to be in that position at such an important moment in my life.

So heading into the game, I felt that if I did well, I'd get a look from major colleges, even the University of Nebraska. I ended up having a good game, and we beat the North team. Bill Dodd, a good friend of mine from Central High, was named outstanding player of the game. It was a great day. I went home to a hero's welcome in my neighborhood.

Everyone around me was curious to see if I'd get offers at that point, and we all were eager to see what the University of Nebraska would do. I have heard people say through the years that the Huskers did come calling to recruit me as an "athlete." If that's true, I knew nothing about that. I never got a call from Nebraska. To this day, I don't know why. Churchich had a good career for the Huskers. And I need to make this clear: I have nothing against Bob Churchich. We've been good friends from age nine on. I respected what he did as a player and who he was as a person. But I was still miffed that Nebraska didn't want me. To this day, they've never acknowledged that they should've recruited me or at least given me a chance. I suppose they had their reasons. And what they've done with black quarterbacks since then is very admirable, especially during the era of Turner Gill, who has since joined the coaching staff, and Tommie Frazier.

At that time, basically, I just had to move on and find a good fit for me, which meant a college that wanted me and would give me a chance to play quarterback.

The state's all-star basketball game was approaching. Again, it featured the best high school players in the state, and I was included. We played against a team that had Nebraska schoolboy legends Fred Hare and Joe Williams. My team was a heavy underdog. Once again, our team won. I was named the Most Valuable Player just one week after upsetting the North in the Shrine Bowl.

I suppose it was the adulation, but I really thought I would get scholarship offers at that point, especially from Nebraska. I thought they'd see my athletic ability in basketball as well as football, having played well against their top recruits in football. That never happened. From what I understand, the reason I didn't get a scholarship to Nebraska was that they knew I was adamant about playing quarterback in college. For obvious reasons, they might not have wanted me to compete against Bob Churchich. To be honest,

I don't know that I would've beaten him out. He obviously did a great job, taking Nebraska to the Orange Bowl. But they skirted the issue by never giving me a chance.

I realized, at that point, that I'd have to lower my hopes in terms of colleges. I started getting more inquiries from smaller schools. As with Nebraska, other Division I schools shied away from me because I wanted to play quarterback. Certainly, Nebraska and those other schools would put black athletes at other positions where they could help out the team, but not at quarterback.

I had two coaches who did recruit me both from Nebraska— Omaha University and Doane College. Bob Rose had been a single-wing quarterback at Omaha University. I had it in the back of my mind that I wanted to go to Omaha University strictly because of Bob Rose. Omaha coach Al Caniglia was relentless recruiting me, and he assured me that I would play quarterback. He also promised me that I would get an education. I told him I wanted to get an engineering degree so I could become an architect. At that time, there was more of an effort nation-wide to put certain athletes in classes that would keep them eligible. At that point, I didn't think that I would become a professional athlete in either basketball or football, so I was mainly concerned with getting my education.

I received partial scholarships for football, basketball and academics. So that took care of almost all of my financial needs for college. It was a good package. They wanted me to play basketball and football. Added with the engineering school, that was a heavy load. I had to make a decision because Doane coach Al Papik was a great man and recruited me with as much vigor as Omaha University. Calling him to tell him I wasn't signing with Doane was one of the hardest calls I ever made. I really respected Coach Papik. Ironically, the University of Nebraska brought Papik into its family a few years later. I commend the Husker program for getting a man of such high ideals and character.

I did look at other small schools in Nebraska and in the Dakotas. But Coach Al's honesty, integrity and personality made Omaha University the best fit.

In the end, I have to thank the University of Nebraska for not recruiting me. Had I signed with the Huskers, I wouldn't have had the chance to become the player I did—likely I wouldn't have played quarterback in college—and made it to the NFL.

Omaha University had an all-American at quarterback that year, Carl Meyers, a local hero. Carl was a senior during my freshman year. So I could learn from a very good quarterback my first year, and then, I reasoned, move to quarterback my sophomore year.

My ego bared its head for the first time. I suppose it popped out to soak in all the limelight I had gotten from the Shrine and basketball all-star games. My first year, I started thinking I was better than I was and that I should be starting ahead of Carl Meyers, which looking back, was ridiculous. The chip on my shoulder was threatening to knock me down several levels. I started believing those around me who said, "You should be the starter." I thought about quitting the team. There's a big lesson there about surrounding yourself with positive people, but not to the extreme that they tell you only what you want to hear—and if they do, the resulting circumstances are your own fault if you believe them.

I had made the varsity my first year, starting on defense at cornerback, which was rare for a freshman back then. And I was the second-string quarterback behind Carl, so I should have been happy. But I was stupid and immature. I decided to skip practice and went to the library. I was ready to quit the team.

Several of my teammates—even Carl Meyers, to show you what kind of man he was down deep—came by to talk to me, to adjust my frame of mind.

"What are you doing?" Carl implored me in the library. "You are going to be the starting quarterback for three years! What more could you want?"

I was way out of line. The coaches wanted me to stay on the team, but they didn't baby me. They talked to me as a young man who was getting bad advice and was about to make a bad decision. I got up from the library table, closed my book and went to practice. From that point forward, I worked harder in practice.

Early that year, we played one of the top-ranked passing teams in the nation, Northern Illinois, at their stadium. They had a great quarterback named George Bork. I intercepted a pass he threw and ran it back for a touchdown. In the previous year's games, George had lit up Omaha U.—and everyone else he played. That touchdown was a rite of passage for me. We did lose that game, but I scored our only touchdown. I ran the ball 10 times that year for 79 yards and completed 4-of-8 passes I threw, as Carl's backup. But I was a starting defensive back, so that was my primary position.

In school, I struggled. I was taking really hard engineering courses. It was quite a load, taking a full class schedule and playing two sports—I was the starting guard on the basketball team, too. All of that, along with getting acclimated to college life and heading into manhood had me scrambling with my time and thoughts. I wanted to explore the other activities on campus, from student government to social issues, but I barely had time each night to make sure I had 10 toes and 10 fingers after doing all I could to complete my academic and athletic commitments.

It was a taxing educational experience and taxing. In 1963, the world was changing. President Kennedy was killed my freshman year while I was taking a physics test. Young Americans were getting killed in Vietnam, a place probably many Americans to this day couldn't find on the globe. Places like Birmingham, Memphis and Little Rock were undergoing racial strife as America struggled with growing pains and acceptances of racial equality.

My horizons began to broaden. I had to make a lot of decisions my freshman year. I had to be not only an athlete, but also a student and maintain some semblance of what was happening in the world. That set the stage for my developing my own philosophy of life, what it takes to make it in life, both on and off the athletic field.

My goal at Omaha U. was to be an architect, which had been my lifelong dream. I also wanted to be a coach and an educator. It was difficult taking all of the engineering courses as a freshman. I was able to get through my freshman year with better than a C average. That was below my expectations. But with football, basketball and everything else, I was simply overwhelmed. Somehow I got through it. I learned a lot about myself during my freshman year. I also took far more credit hours than the standard student-athlete would take.

I looked forward to extending the success I had experienced as a freshman to my sophomore year.

Carl Meyers was graduating and it was up to me to carry on the torch at quarterback. Carl had been a heck of a quarterback. Though I never wavered and never thought about failure, the challenge was substantial on the field.

My primary focus, however, was still academics. Omaha University at the time didn't have an architectural program, so I planned to go on to the University of Nebraska after graduating from Omaha U., because Nebraska had a very good architectural program.

Gale Sayers' brother, Roger, had helped shape me as a student-athlete my freshman year. Roger was a world-class sprinter and good football player, especially as a kick returnee. I had played with or against him and Gale since midget football. My freshman year, Roger always sat next to me. He was a senior and took me under his wing. I was impressed that Roger always had a book, was always reading or studying. That rubbed off on me, to see how in-tune he was with his academic commitments. Roger would have made it to the NFL and been a star like Gale had he ever gotten bigger physically; I believe he never weighed much more than 150 or 160 pounds.

It also got my attention when the Green Bay Packers drafted one of the players from my freshman year, Jack Petersen. That validated our competitive level and showed that players from our division could make it to the "next level."

I worked hard in the summer honing my football and basketball skills.

My sophomore year was a very tumultuous year.

In football, we had some great players coming back to the team. Gerald Allen, who would make Little All-American, was back. So was Jimmy Jones, a tight end who would go on to the NFL and then become an accomplished businessman.

It was time for me to take over the offense as a sophomore. We had a pretty good team that year, and some great players. But we had lost a lot of great players from the previous team. I threw for 939 yards, completing 73 of 143 passes, was intercepted nine times, and tossed nine touchdowns. I ran 127 times for 370 yards.

We had a so-so season, finishing 6-5. I began to get some accolades as a quarterback. I had, as expected, some up-and-down games. The games that I did excel in were exceptional for my size, stature and limited experience as a starter. That was an exciting period, to be starting quarterback for Omaha University. Coaches like Don Watchorn and Ken Fischer did all they could to encourage me. Ken was a very stern tactician, who had been my defensive coach my freshman year. He always knew when to press the buttons. He had a subtle sense of humor. It all added up to a great coach and great communicator.

Al Caniglia was not only my coach during my college days, but also kind of like a father figure to me. He had done his homework recruiting me, and knew about my family. He gave me the opportunity to play the position I wanted. So I never wanted to let him down.

Something very odd happened during that year. We opened the season in a night game at Rosenblatt Stadium against Idaho State. At the beginning of the game I threw two passes to Ulysses Cribbs, or Butch, as I called him, who was like a brother to me growing up. For some reason, Butch was very nervous before the game. He had seemed to become more detached from society the previous year or so.

We had spent a lot of time working out the previous summer for the upcoming season and we were still close, but I felt him slipping away—but what it meant, I didn't know.

We had been teammates together as freshmen for basketball and football. I couldn't put my finger on it—perhaps because my focus was on the game—but something was noticeably wrong with Butch that day. He dropped those first two passes. Coach Caniglia had to take him out of the game. In the heat of battle, I didn't really give it a second thought. We ended up losing the game, and I could see that Butch blamed himself. But those drops happened early and ended up not affecting the game. We simply got beat that day.

The game ended Saturday night and I didn't see Butch at school on Monday. I didn't see him at football practice that day, either, which really sent off an alarm. We usually talked every day, and I hadn't seen him since the game. I went to his mother's house in North Omaha after football practice that evening.

His mother looked solemn. She had been crying.

"Where is Butch?" I asked her when she opened the door.

"Butch," she said quietly, "joined the service."

He was going to Vietnam. I had a very, very bad feeling about that. Butch's future, which was supposed to include three more

years of football and a college education—the "best" years of our
lives, as the college experience has been dubbed—was now irrevo-
cably changed. And he had just picked up and headed to Vietnam
to fight a war? It didn't make sense. I would not hear from Butch
for several years. And the next time I did, the news would get even
worse.

Though football didn't go as well as it could, it was still a good
season. Academically, I plodded along, but school was tough.

Football season overlapped basketball season. I moved right
into basketball as football wound down. Our coach, Jim Borsheim,
was a very quirky guy. He depended on me to be the guard. We had
good players, but never the kind of team we should have had with
that talent. It was a unique mix of older players back from the service, and an ethnic/racial melting pot, so that put some pressure on
Coach Borsheim.

For the first time, I became discouraged in basketball. My play
was erratic. I had a lot of lab classes for engineering, which were at
night after basketball practice. I was constantly fatigued physically
and mentally. My battery was wearing down. I trudged on and got
through it. I still wasn't in great shape academically, but based on
my challenging schedule and sports, just making it through was a
victory in itself.

I still had to work part-time, and full-time in the summertime.
Many of us worked in the packinghouses. That was really hard
work. I'd tone the hides full of salt, shaking the heavy hides. We had
a hide cellar that had huge rats. It was a dark, wet place. We'd prepare the hides with salt, clip them and process them. When we'd
work on hogs, it was equally as tough. We had to process the pork
with a really hot furnace. I'd get dehydrated and get cramps. But
that was important money that I really needed.

During my sophomore and junior years, I worked for a county
surveyor named Bill Green. I was a draftsman, and I loved that job.
I learned a lot about engineering and construction. That was one of
my better jobs because it applied to my goal of being an architect,
and I had taken drafting courses in college.

I trained hard in the summer entering my junior year. Again,
several of our players, including Gerald Allen, were drafted to the
pros. Since I was one of the better players on the team, in the back

of my mind I quietly entertained the notion that I might get a chance to try out for a pro team. I didn't take it that seriously at that point, but it did change my approach to working out and improving. I had grown some and gotten physically stronger.

I played basketball on the playgrounds against some great players, including Creighton's Paul Silas and held my own. My main priority was getting through engineering school and getting to the University of Nebraska to architectural school.

The water started seeping out over the top of my glass my junior year. Academics were intensifying and something had to give. One of the sports would have to fall victim so I could finish my primary obligation and goal of getting an education. Though I loved basketball, it was secondary at that point because of how I felt for Coach Al. I didn't make the decision at that point, but I had a feeling I was going to have to deal with it.

With my mind in better shape, I had a good junior year, and our team improved. I ran for 513 yards on 120 carries, and completed 116 of 206 passes for 1,668 yards, for a total of 2,181 yards of total offense, over 800 yards more than my sophomore year. That set a school record for total offense. We finished 8-2 that year, a great year for Omaha University, and the excitement around the football program was reaching new levels.

My own play was better, more importantly, so was the play of our team. We beat some good teams and took some noted teams to the wire. I made all-Central Intercollegiate Conference and got some recognition, even some national exposure.

"Marlin Briscoe" did not sound like a black name, and Omaha University was not a primarily black college. We didn't have highlights on national TV like they do these days. All the national media could go by was your statistics, and the teams you played against. What I'm saying is that not a lot of people knew Marlin Briscoe was a black quarterback. When I'd meet people—scouts, coaches, other players from other areas—I'd invariably hear, "Hey, I didn't know you were black." That would happen for the next 12 years or so.

Still, I realized I was starting to get looked at, perhaps ever so slightly by professional football teams. That affected my thought process. I suddenly realized I had to continue to improve athletically. Up to that point, athletics had been mainly a means to get through college and get that education. Slowly but surely, I was thinking I could do what some of the other guys on my team—and guys I was playing against—were doing: play professional football. I wasn't saying that I was better than those guys who had made it to the pros were. But I at least held my own, so to me, that meant I had a chance.

I was aware that being both black and "small for a quarterback" might work against me. But I had refuted the naysayers from midget football through college, so I started to think, "I could make it to the pros and overcome those stereotypes again."

As basketball season started, I was already exhausted. It was not fun. We weren't winning and there was utter chaos within the team, with conflicts between coaches and players. Prior to that season, basketball had been my favorite sport. Halfway through the season, I realized that I had been right in late summer, thinking I would have to give up one of the sports. Basketball was going poorly, and my schoolwork was more challenging than ever. My courses were tough and more technical than ever. I could no longer juggle school and two sports. So I did what would have previously been the unthinkable: I quit the basketball team to focus on my studies.

Though I felt badly walking away from the team, that was one of the better decisions I ever made because I was able to get my grade-point average higher than it had ever been. I would go study instead of rushing to basketball practice. I'd get home in the evening to study and I'd still have energy, even if I had to work that day. There wasn't as much of a strain on time, and the lack of stress improved my mental outlook. I could also concentrate solely on football conditioning and workouts, which would allow me to better showcase my talents to scouts my senior year.

Ironically, basketball—though I had left the team midway through my junior year—would nearly end my athletic career in the months to come.

And life was still changing for blacks.

In 1966, we had some racial confrontations in Omaha, right after the horrible race riots in Watts, which drew national and worldwide attention. I was starting to drive home in Omaha one night from school. I went past Memorial Park and saw the police beating this black kid. I didn't want to see this kid, who looked about 15 years old, killed, so I stopped my car. Everything was coming to a head, in my own mind as well as nationwide. I got out of my car, and one of the police officers saw me.

"What's going on?" I asked.

"Move on!" he yelled.

I kept walking toward him. He came over and knocked me down, kneeing me in the back and hitting me with his baton several times. For some reason, I remember seeing the college's football stadium before I ran into the police officer—a stadium where I was being applauded just months early and would be again in weeks—yet here I was not far from there, being beaten like a dog who had wet the carpet.

The cop ended up running me off, back to my car, but I had accomplished my goal, because they stopped beating the black kid. I'll never forget that incident and the feelings that I was experiencing.

6

Broken Neck, Shattered Dreams

Basketball was still part of my summer regimen for staying in shape. It was the summer of 1966, and I was very excited for football to start, even after the beating weeks earlier at the hands of the cop.

My life and the reality of what can happen in one moment in sports were about to collide. Only one would survive.

Or, perhaps more fatefully, neither would.

There was only one week before my senior college school year started. I was notified that there was a youth center opening in North Omaha, and they were having a charity/celebrity basketball game to christen the opening. Quite a few well-known area athletes were participating, and since it was to help kids—I remember what the Woodson Center did for me growing up—I had no inkling of saying no.

Besides, my good buddy Johnny Alexander was playing in that game, on my team, as it turned out. Johnny had played college basketball at Peru State in Nebraska and had gone on to play for a professional touring team.

I shouldn't have taken that chance of playing in that game.

Before the game, I remember seeing a guy on the other team who was known to be a sort of dirty player. He had hurt players before—I had heard stories, at least. I kind of shook off the thought, and got ready for the game. I was having fun, and the game was very competitive. I went up high to block his shot, and the guy known as a dirty player proved it. He undercut me—Johnny Alexander tried unsuccessfully to catch me as I somersaulted to the floor—and I landed headfirst.

The feeling was gone in my arms and legs. I was out cold for several minutes. When I came to, my limbs were numb, completely.

I thought I was paralyzed.

My neck had snapped back dangerously. The feeling came back eventually, and I was taken to the hospital. The pain was starting to settle in hours later as I waited for the doctor after having several tests done.

I expected the worst news possible, hoping for the best.

"Really," the doctor told me, "I couldn't find anything."

What a relief, I thought to myself.

"But I was paralyzed for a few minutes," I said. "My neck, it snapped back. I lost the feeling in my arms and legs."

" I couldn't find anything," the doctor said with a shrug.

I was given a clean bill of health to go back to football practice.

What luck, I thought to myself. My neck was stiff, though, so I missed a few practices. I only came back for the final couple of practices before the first game of the 1966 season against Idaho State, a good NCAA team that Omaha U. had added to beef up the schedule.

My neck wasn't right; I knew that much. I also knew my team needed me for this big game. Plus, the doctor had cleared me.

I had a huge game, but we lost to heavily favored Idaho State. Late in the game, I got hit and felt a pop in my neck. I wobbled to the sideline and didn't go back in the game. When I got home, I ended up seeing a doctor who I hadn't met before. He came into the room and looked at me, holding up an X-ray.

"You have a vertebra in your neck that is fractured," he said. "You shouldn't even have been playing!"

I was shocked. He looked at the X-ray and could tell that it hadn't happened that night but a week ago.

"Do you realize that you could have ended up a paraplegic if you were hit at just a slightly different angle?" the doctor asked.

"I didn't even know I had a fractured bone," I answered. "I was cleared to play by another doctor last week."

The doctor shook his head.

"That was an incorrect diagnosis. Your season is over," he said, patting me on the knee.

"I can live with that," I said. "There's always next year."

The doctor looked toward the ground. He was standing. He sat down and put his hands on my forearms.

"You won't play football again," he said. "The risk for paralysis is way, way too high, too severe. I'm sorry, son."

The air was out of my lungs. I couldn't cry because I was numb. I looked at him.

"Never again," the doctor said compassionately. "I'm sorry. But you are fortunate. This could have been much worse. If you'd have continued playing, it would be much worse—just one hit, and that would have been it. Not just for football, but life as you know it. You would be in a wheelchair, and best-case scenario, you'd have use of your arms, if you were lucky."

Football was, in a lot of ways, life as I knew it. Twenty-four hours earlier I had been getting ready for the biggest college game of my life. Now these doctors were telling me it was the last game of my life.

"This is what they call a 'career-ending' injury," the doctor said. "It is, virtually, a broken neck, Marlin."

I realized in that moment that sports was but a fleeting moment in life. It can all be taken away in a second. I went from all-American to the sidelines. My career was over. I would not play sports at a competitive level ever again. All for getting cut on a cheap shot in a charity basketball game.

Obviously, I had to abandon my first dream of playing professional football and another dream of playing professional basketball—something, because of my deep belief in myself, I thought would be possible, even if I ended up making it in professional football.

My perspective changed as quickly as a snap of the fingers. Or in this case, with the popping of a neck. As I sat there, I turned my thoughts to schoolwork. I was in college to get an education. All of my concentration would be on that.

I left the hospital and did a lot of soul-searching. The well wishes and friends offered support, but they couldn't understand—try as they might—what I was going through. The warmth of the spotlight was gone, and the cold of the shadows was chilling my aching bones.

The team struggled, winning only one game during the entire 1966 season. That 1-9 record was a huge disappointment considering the 8-2 success of 1965.

I had 18 credit hours, the maximum full academic load, and three hours above what was considered "full-time" student status. But the pain from the fractured vertebra, along with the incredibly painful, time-consuming treatment was too much for me to do all the studying.

So I did the logical thing, dropping six credit hours, realizing 12 could be manageable. I went to treatment, and got on with my life.

And then, one day, the mail came with a notice I hadn't expected.

This period of time was during the Vietnam War, and anyone in college enrolled in fewer than 15 credit hours was eligible for the Vietnam draft. Certainly, I thought that wouldn't apply to me because I had a broken neck.

Surprise, surprise, I opened the letter, and it was a draft notice. I still didn't entertain the notion that a young man with a broken neck could be drafted.

Still, that was the law—that I'd have to take the physical—so off I went. To my amazement, I passed the physical with a broken neck! I was told I would be headed for basic training, and likely Vietnam, within the year.

My community—friends, neighbors, the university—were outraged. But in those days, the Army was taking anyone. I suppose the attitude was "If you can walk, you can die." And I could, after all, walk.

I was able to get a second physical before I had to go to the draft board. I was told to bring "a toothbrush, and a change of undershirt and underwear in preparation to be shipped out" once I passed the physical.

Thankfully, I failed the second physical.

I continued to develop other interests since my sports career was over. There were social issues in my neighborhood. I changed my major to education, so I had to line up plans to student teach. I also ran for student government. That was an important election for me.

Student council in college was a great experience. Getting elected was rewarding because a lot of my black peers had encouraged me to run because the country was in such racial turmoil. Though some might see it as "only a college election," I viewed it as running for all of the blacks in our community as well as at the college. I knew we needed to be more visible and not take more subservient positions when higher office was available if only we had the courage to pursue it. In that regard, the black population at school to run for the student council handpicked me.

We had a lot of white kids at Omaha University, so I really didn't think I had a chance. I know it wasn't because I was a jock. I mean, there was no more "geeky" looking guy than me, with my slide rule and T-square in my pocket every day for engineering school. I took the bus—actually two because I had to make a connection—to and from school, so I wasn't a high roller by any means. Just an everyday Joe, hoping to make a difference.

After I won election to office, I was stunned to hear that I was the first black to hold such a post at the university.

Really, I was finding my niche. I loved student government because I was able to enact the wishes of those who had elected me. I knew what it was like as a black not to be represented or have my views matter. This was a chance to put my money where my mouth was and step up to the plate. So I did.

As blacks, we were troubled by what was happening in the South. We saw a lot of blacks getting bitten by dogs, sprayed by fire hoses, and even killed. Here we were with a lot of the same racism, but not the violence that the Southern states were suffering through. The racism we experienced was more discriminatory, whether it was in the job sector or in admission to certain places that were for whites only, either implied or applied.

There was a park in West Omaha—that has since been torn down—named Peony Park. It was a neat place, with a man-made beach and everything, just a really fun place. Again, it was one of those places that was deemed to be, although not officially, for whites only. Blacks had always wanted to go there. So a bunch of us on the student council, probably 12 of us, decided to go to Peony Park. There was no confrontation at all. They let us in, we swam and had a good time, and we went home.

It was during that time that I also found my first love, Miss Beverly Wright, who was the first Miss Black Nebraska. I found there were other things in life besides sports. Keep in mind that this whole school year, the fall of 1966 to the spring of 1967, I was 100 percent certain I would never play sports again. My focus to explore and develop other interests, and to discover new things, was very strong.

Treatment and therapy continued with two doctors, Dr. Fischer and Dr. Jensen. I did something else after hurting my neck; I was an undergraduate assistant coach for the rest of the football season. It was so hard to watch virtually the same team I had quarterbacked to an 8-2 record the year before, win just once and finish 1-9. I felt worse for Coach Al, because he put so much into that season and hopes were so high. I could see the hurt and disappointment in Coach Al's eyes at practice.

That spurred my interest in coaching. I felt this calling was one I could certainly live with after having sports taken away so suddenly, so permanently.

I kept plugging away, finishing up my academic work. I passed my Kappa Alpha Psi test, to join that black fraternity—white fraternities at that time didn't accept blacks, so we had just two black frats from which to choose.

Late in the school year, life was going well—student council, academics, time with Miss Beverly, volunteering, the fraternity— then I had something strange happen.

My doctors, Fischer and Jensen, checked me out as per our regularly scheduled exam, part of the entire rehabilitation/therapy program. They called me to come back just a couple of days later, the week before summer break. I worried that there was a problem they had discovered while looking at the results of the tests and X-rays they had done two days earlier.

"Marlin, come on in, sit down," Dr. Jensen said.

Both of the men were excellent—outstanding—doctors, and I was still assuming the worst. But since I had great doctors, at least I would get the proper diagnosis and proper treatment—or surgery—if need be.

"Your neck is starting to re-calcify," Dr. Fischer said. "The X-ray clearly shows that. This doesn't happen often, Marlin."

"That's right," Dr. Jensen said. "Very rare, Marlin."

"So this is a good thing, I'm assuming," I said, unsure of what the implications were.

The two men stood up, and for some reason, so did I.

"Marlin," Dr. Fischer asked, "do you realize what this means?"

"Well…actually—no," I answered.

"It means," Dr. Jensen said, "that you'll be able to play football again."

I sat back down. The air was back in my lungs. I felt moisture in my eyes. I could see the joy in the eyes of the doctors who had given me such good care, seemingly as happy for me as I was for myself.

The road back would not be an easy one, though. I had lost a lot of strength and conditioning, obviously, because of the neck injury.

So what?

It was time to rock and time to roll. Time to start chasing my original dream. I went and talked to Coach Al, and he looked like he could walk on the ceiling.

I still wasn't close to graduating because I had switched majors. I had enough credits to graduate, but not enough in my major, which was now education.

Looking back, I believe the neck injury was a blessing. It forced me to do something I would not have otherwise done; look outside of the world of sports for sustenance, hope and a future. Though that was my toughest year at college, I still count it as arguably my best and clearly the most rewarding, from student government to the fraternity and everything else. I liked the way my world had opened up. I traveled down roads I never knew existed.

It all comes back to a fundamental principle: Everything is what we make it to be, no more and no less. In that regard, I'm glad I didn't go into a shell because of the injury. On the other hand, I wish it hadn't taken such an injury to get me to explore the world a little more.

And I still viewed sports as a fleeting moment. Sure, my neck was healing completely. But I knew I had to be a renaissance person no matter what—I had to have hobbies, develop interests outside of sports. I knew that I could go out for football again and have it all end in one play.

That lesson served me well not only at that time, but later in life. Knowing that it could all disappear in a split second gave me new life and inspired me with my preparation for the upcoming season.

Since I hadn't played in three games in 1966, I could apply for a hardship case. The NAIA (now the NCAA presides over Omaha U., which is now the University of Nebraska-Omaha) gave me another year of eligibility. I prepared with great zealousness to get in shape and honed my skills. I worked harder than ever before because I had a second chance. I wonder if people realize what a second chance is: It's really nothing more than hope, but hope is a great gift. Before I needed a second chance, I had absolutely no grasp that things could be taken away so quickly and so cruelly. If you get a second chance, by all means jump on it with all your physical and mental might.

It also made me study harder because I knew I would need the education to fall back on at some point—which was very clear. So as I got back to pursuing my dream of playing pro football, I was already the poster child for having an education to fall back on, and I wasn't about to forget that.

My "second" senior season was incredible. It could have been better, but it was a good year, nonetheless. I put up good numbers, and left school with 22 records, from total offense to passing, for individual seasons, and career. The Omaha University sports information department did a great job promoting me, coining "Marlin the Magician" before my "first senior year" and then dusting that promotional material off to help procure a lot of national attention, which only added to my chances of both all-American honors and getting a good look from professional football.

I really didn't know my career numbers (they were researched for this book), and since I don't really like blowing my own horn, here is an excerpt provided by Nebraska-Omaha following my playing days under the headline, "Mr. Quarterback-Marlin Briscoe":

"Probably the greatest all-around football player in the University's gridiron history has to be the 1967 NAIA All-American Quarterback, Marlin Briscoe. This amazing little field general, now with the Denver Broncos of the AFL, led Omaha teams to a combined mark of 27-11-0 during the four years that he played. Briscoe has his name in the Omaha record book 22 times, with totals that may never be broken by a future Omaha player.

"The 5-10, 170-pound former Omaha South star capped a brilliant career in 1967 with a record-smashing 356 yards passing and 401 yards in total offense against powerful North Dakota State. His 2,283 passing yards (for the season) gained him the number seven spot among NAIA schools across the nation, while his total offense figure of 263.9 yards per game placed him fifth nationally.

"The game against North Dakota State, a losing 41-33 effort against the nation's number two rated college division team, probably was Briscoe's greatest effort in many great ones. He threw 28 times and completed 18 for 356 yards and four touchdowns. In addition, he rolled up 45 yards rushing in a superhuman effort against the touted Bison. When he left the game with just 30 seconds to go after passing for his fourth touchdown, the crowd of 6,017 gave him a standing ovation.

"In the season finale against South Dakota, the amazing senior threw three touchdown passes and completed 19 of 34 passes for 275 yards against the Coyotes. His efforts did not go without notice. Four weeks later, he was named the NAIA All-American quarterback on the first team, and to the Michigan Chronicle's All-American Negro Team backfield along with LeRoy Keyes of Purdue, O.J. Simpson of Southern California, and Lee White of Weber State. To top it off, Briscoe was drafted 14th by the Denver Broncos in the annual collegiate player draft by professional football clubs."

To me, the big thing my senior year is that we won the Central Intercollegiate Conference. That was a big feather in Coach Al's cap. He deserved it. Plus, this was with a team that was 1-9 the year before.

I was fortunate to make second team Small All-American behind Greg Landry, who would become a friend and teammate years later in the NFL.

By then, pro football—the AFL, NFL and Canadian Football League—was obviously taking notice of me.

But there was still work to do at Omaha University. Closing an important circle—basketball, was important to me. After all, I considered basketball my first love and a good part of my life. Ironically, I was injured playing basketball, never football. I felt like I had to play again to show I could get back on the court. But there was another reason.

I had quit midway through my junior year. Though my reasoning was well thought out, secure and easily justifiable—I needed the time for school, the team was in chaos—I had still walked off a job that was incomplete. It left a circle that needed to be closed. To walk out under those circumstances—though it was the correct decision at the time—wasn't me.

So I thought about what was facing me down the road in a couple of months. I was headed for pro football, where the turmoil could be huge at times, and where I'd have to fight through chaos and adversity. I had to overcome all of those phobias before I could go to the next level, professional football.

Much to the surprise of Coach Borsheim, I went out for the team my senior year. That I felt he was a difficult coach to play for was only that much more reason to go out for the team again. After all, I was certain I'd face a tough coach in pro football. So I'd be missing an opportunity if I didn't go back out for the team and learn to find my place and survive with a coach I viewed as difficult. There's no shame in "swimming with the tide."

You don't have to—and shouldn't—give up your principles or values. But if you constantly "swim against the tide" just for your own selfish reasons, you will get nowhere in life. I learned perseverance and patience that senior year of basketball.

There were still a lot of ups and downs on that team. The problems surfaced, as they had before—and as I had expected them to again. But I handled them the right way my senior year. I wasn't a regular starter, and I didn't see a lot of playing time every game. But I didn't pout, and I didn't walk away. I saw things through and thus developed a sense of resiliency I hadn't before discovered within myself.

I played for what I suppose could be called "selfish" reasons—not to score points or be a hero—but to grasp the concept of surviving adversity and putting ego aside. I wanted to be a part of that team and at the same time prove something to myself: that I could stick it out when the going got tough—that I would be tougher when the situation called for that kind of character. I had to bite my tongue at times. That's all right because that is part of life. That season was a great learning experience.

The Denver Broncos came to several of those basketball games, just to see my athletic ability and perhaps what I was like as a leader. After basketball season, the Broncos drafted me in the 14th round.

There was still trouble ahead in ways I never could have anticipated. Driving to class on April 4, 1968, I turned on the radio. As I pulled into the campus parking lot, the music was interrupted for a news bulletin.

"Civil Rights leader Martin Luther King, Jr. was shot and killed," the voice said.

I went numb. Martin Luther King had been assassinated. I sat and cried, just sobbing uncontrollably. I couldn't go to class with that news on my mind. I went home and got on the phone to my friends. All of the blacks in the project—blacks everywhere—were devastated. It knocked me over. I had been on campus taking a physics test when news came that President Kennedy was shot five years earlier, and on campus again when Martin Luther King was gunned down.

Dr. King's legacy wasn't about being a man of color. It was about fairness, living in harmony and moving forward. This country still isn't anywhere close to having a black for its President. And many of us believe that if a black somehow got elected, there would be an assassination very quickly. I believe Colin Powell declined running for President because he knows that there would be that fraction out there trying to kill him. This country has always been slow to accept black leaders. We are still dreadfully slow even to have blacks head corporations or other leadership posts. Black leadership in sports has been slow.

I respect Dr. King because he overcame so much. He knew the pain we had endured, and were enduring. We were brought over in chains to this country and in the timeline of human life, it wasn't that long ago. Dr. King did things the right way, with a peaceful agenda. That was unreal and inspiring because he wanted fairness, respect and equality for all people, not just blacks. Blacks were screaming, "No more!" Yet Dr. King was able to lead and try and get these people with different ideologies and philosophies to realize we can all live together in harmony. He wanted to help Asians, Hispanics, handicapped people, and women—everyone who was facing discrimination and prejudice. He faced danger every day and stood up in what was then an especially violent era, facing down unfathomable obstacles. In that regard, I believe Dr. King changed the entire complexion of the world. At that time, a radical segment of society wanted to cut out the heart, lungs and soul of his movement, figuring that was the way to kill it, particularly the black race.

Though Dr. King was murdered that day, no one could ever eliminate his spirit. The day had passed for that because his legacy and philosophy were established. The seeds had been planted and had spread at the time of his murder.

7

Creating a Place for History in Denver

After the Broncos drafted me, Bronco scout Stan Jones and Denver's Director of Personnel Fred Gerhke came to Omaha to sign me.

I was prepared for that meeting, so much so that I believe I surprised–maybe even shocked–both men.

You see, I knew the Broncos weren't looking at me as a quarterback. But I had a dream of getting a shot at quarterback. Into the picture once again stepped Al Caniglia.

Coach Al, who knew the ins and outs of pro ball from his playing days, spoon-fed me some good information and advice. In those days, the formula for signing a player was pretty cut and dry, so much so that agents weren't needed. There was a fixed–and rather paltry or minuscule compared to today's exorbitant salaries–amount of money and terms. So Coach Al suggested rather than go the agent route, and lose a percentage of money to the agent, that I negotiate my own contract.

"The Broncos are one of the few teams in pro ball that have their training camp open to the public and media," Coach Al told me in a private meeting. "You know what that means? It means you can showcase your talent, and people other than the coaches and personnel directors will see."

Coach Al knew I wanted to play quarterback. I knew there were no black quarterbacks in pro ball–none had ever started a game in the AFL or NFL to that point–so I thought my chances were slim. Coach Al had some advice.

"You can negotiate your own contract," Coach Al said, "and stipulate that you get a tryout at quarterback. Denver, like a lot of other teams, brings in its quarterbacks before the rest of the players for mini-camp to learn the offense. So it wouldn't interfere with their plans for you as a defensive back."

I went to dinner armed with this great information. Jones and Gerhke outlined their plans for me.

"We think you're good enough, Marlin, to step right in and start at cornerback for us," Fred said. "We will have an all rookie defensive secondary, and that will include you."

I nodded, and was grateful for both their belief in me and the chance to play professional football. It was my turn to speak.

"Thank you, I'm very excited to join the Broncos," I told them. "And I will acquiesce to your wish to play cornerback. I look forward to playing that position for your team. I'll come to training camp ready to be a cornerback. But there is one thing I will insist upon."

The two men looked at me at bit puzzled.

"I will play cornerback, however, I want it written into my contract that I will get a three-day tryout at quarterback," I said. "At the end of that period, I will switch to cornerback and I have no problem with that. I'm not a troublemaker and I don't want to make waves. I just want the tryout."

Both men were reluctant, but I was adamant. I did have an ace in the hole–and both Denver men knew it–and that was the Canadian Football League, which had expressed a big interest in me. That leverage was enough, apparently.

To appease me, and maybe even to let me get that dream of being a quarterback out of my system, they let me write that into the contract.

I could almost hear the rumblings in Denver when that contract was showed to Broncos Coach Lou Saban. His hands were tied; he had to give me a chance for that three-day tryout. Without that little clause in my contract, I would never have had the chance to make history as the first black quarterback to start and play regularly for a professional football team.

Playing for the Broncos excited me. I was going to realize my lifelong dream of playing pro football. The AFL was better than the NFL for me because the AFL had a track record of being liberal in the opportunities it gave to black players. The NFL was regarded by many in the African-American athletic community as limiting the number of blacks who could try out, and make its teams.

The AFL was only eight years old at that point and was more open-minded about black athletes. So I knew that was my best opportunity in 1968. The AFL wasn't considered on par with the NFL by some in the media.

That wasn't true at all.

And it proved to be more than the NFL's equal the next year when the AFL beat the NFL's team in the Super Bowl.

So I had my contract and my big chance. However, my path to making the Broncos and getting a foothold in professional football was far from assured even at that point.

I had a lot of work to do that summer, getting prepared for my quarterback tryout while learning more about how to play defensive back, something I hadn't done since my freshman year at Omaha University.

I also had to get the conditioning it would take to play at the sport's highest professional level. I ran hills and lifted weights. I did a lot of backpedaling and throwing. I had to "learn how to run"— the technique of which has only gotten really big and trendy the last 10 years, as players have pushed the edge of the physical-limitations envelope.

Though I was quick, I was never fast, never one of those guys who could just fly up and down the field past everyone. Being a quarterback at Omaha, I never really had to have straight-ahead speed. I had to "learn how to run" in a short period of time. I worked out three times a day.

That summer was intense. One workout would be primarily at quarterback. Then I'd do a workout at defensive back. The other workout was for speed, strength and endurance. I trained like I never had before. Sometimes I trained by myself. But a lot of times, the guys I grew up with and played with in college were there to help me. I could always find a guy to throw passes to. I could always find a guy to defend against. The guys from the semi-pro team, the Omaha Mustangs, would show up at the park and I would throw to them, or they would run routes and I would cover them.

I still played basketball for conditioning, too. Really, I just immersed myself to prepare for the tryouts. I also learned another valuable lesson about over-training. I strained my body so much that I developed hamstring problems that would haunt me throughout my career.

Going to the Broncos' training camp in the late summer of 1968 was an exciting thing for me. I received some publicity from my success as a college quarterback. But I was given almost no chance at playing quarterback because of my size and because I was competing in a realm that had always consisted of white quarterbacks.

There were eight quarterbacks in camp. And what do you know: It was the same scenario that had occurred in midget football. I truly had a feeling of déjà vu as all of Denver's quarterback hopefuls were placed ahead of me for the various drills.

Steve Tensi was Denver's starter, and he was one of the best quarterbacks in the league. I liked Steve immensely, and he would quickly become a life-long friend, confidante, and supporter.

We had two-a-day practices to start out, which consisted of learning plays and studying playbooks. Most of the drills were about footwork and throwing skills. We progressed to the workout of passing. Now, I had come to grips with the likelihood that I wasn't going to get a fair shake. I was prepared for that. I knew that mentally I had to be tough because I knew how it was going to unfold. I had to remember my senior year playing basketball for Omaha U.–and to keep that calm and resiliency, to solve the problem of the injustice that would occur. All I could do was perform and not let my emotions get in the way of how I would perform.

Each quarterback was supposed to get 10 short-range, 10 medium-range and 10 long-range throws. All of the other quarterbacks had their throws. Since I was the last one, I'd end up getting just five throws, then, "Hey let's go to the next drill" and I would get shorted. I was the only one who didn't get to complete the drills. I was prepared for that though, knowing that would be the case. I made sure every throw I made was my best throw. Eyes were still upon me even though I wasn't going to get a fair amount of throws and evaluation from the coaching staff. The ace up my sleeve was that the media and fans were watching.

The long-range throws were the big surprise for everyone watching. Steve Tensi was about 6-foot-5, 220 pounds. He had played at Florida State and thrown to Fred Biletnikoff in college. So he had the big-time school among his credentials. People–myself included–loved to watch him throw with that big arm in Denver's thin air, where the ball seemed to carry forever. He was the proto-typical big-time quarterback. I was in awe of Steve because his passes were a beautiful thing to see. And he was pretty accurate.

Finally, it was my turn to throw the long-range passes and I fully expected an abbreviated performance. So I made a calculated decision. We were throwing to receivers downfield–no pass rush or anything, just seeing how accurate we were. To make the biggest possible impression, I would wait until the receivers were viewed as "out of reach" and I'd throw it as far, or farther, than Tensi, and right on the money. People were shocked. I could even hear the "oohs and aahs." They couldn't believe a guy my size could throw it that far. I wasn't surprised. This was part of my plan, to prove my point that I could throw the ball far and accurate. The first time the coaches saw that, they quickly shut down the drill and said, "Let's go do something else."

I'd smile inside because I knew I was doing my best. The next drill was footwork. This was where I really excelled. In those days, quarterbacks were different. Steve was strictly a drop-back quarter-back. But Denver had problems on the offensive line, so they real-ly needed someone who could offset that problem with some mobility. Part of the quarterback's job was to handle the ball and get out of binds when the blocking broke down–to escape the danger and still make the play. Of course, the coaches were looking for that from everyone except me–I was on a tryout I wiggled into, and then they could get me out of their hair and onto the other side of the ball.

However, those footwork drills were where I really stood out. Again, I was given the least amount of chances. I could run and throw right on the money whereas the other quarterbacks were pretty much strictly drop-back passers. I'd cunningly roll out left and throw across the field to my right side, right on the money. Then I'd go right and throw left, again right on the money. That was something difficult to do. Most of the quarterbacks couldn't do that at all, and none close to as well as I did it. I was getting some attention for doing it—people were watching. I'd stay after practice and do it some more. All the fans and media would watch, and I could hear the whispers and praise.

But the coaches didn't whisper. All I heard was, "Hurry up, get to the showers"—anything to get me off the field. Though it sounds like I was being selfish—and I was, in all honesty, doing it for my own purpose—I wasn't doing it to show up anyone else. I hadn't gotten my fair number of repetitions, so I was evening it out with the after-practice throws.

The receivers, much, I expect, to the chagrin of the coaches, loved it. They would gladly stay after and work with me. It quickly became evident to the fans and media that the black quarterback from Omaha had at least the physical skills and mental aptitude to earn a chance to play quarterback at this level. I call that whole scenario my "immaculate deception," and it paid off because I had an audience.

At the end of the three-day tryout, the Denver media gave me great coverage. I'd hear things from the press like, "Too bad you're a cornerback because you did so well." That still made me feel good.

But the three days ended. Lou Saban had fulfilled the contract clause and quickly sent me to my position on defense. The press asked Saban several times about me. I didn't hear his response, but when I was asked by the press if I'd pursue quarterback, I tried to handle it with dignity and class.

"I was given a three-day tryout," I answered. "I'll compete as a defensive back from now on."

No fanfare, no complaints from me. I knew in my heart that I had performed well enough to compete for the job at quarterback. I had done what I set out to do. I had no real illusions of playing quarterback in professional football. But I was smug about having outsmarted them and letting them know that a black man could clearly play quarterback at that level. My view was that if I weren't going to create a spot for myself, then maybe in some small way I'd create a door for a black quarterback to come through the next year or down the road.

The rest of the players came into camp, and I had to focus quickly on competing. The bump-and-run play at defensive back was new to me. I worked extra hard. I played well enough in exhibition games to become a starter at right cornerback.

Then something happened. I pulled a hamstring. I had finally made it–starting as a rookie, and I got hurt. I felt I had let the organization and myself down. I came back too soon and pulled it again. And again. I did not know the depths of what a hamstring pull could do to you because I had never had one before. I wanted to do my job and keep my position as a rookie starter at a position I hadn't really played much.

But things happen in life. The fact that I got hurt was probably one of the best things that ever happened to me, though it was by no conceivable means intentional.

The Broncos waited me out and let me heal, but we were quickly nearing the end of the exhibition season. Another cornerback was elevated ahead of me to start.

While I was on the mend, the offense was having a lot of difficulty scoring. In fact, the offense didn't score in our final two exhibition games. My friend Steve Tensi suffered a broken collarbone. I hurt for Steve because he was the man, and he had clearly earned his place. He was Denver's franchise player, and losing him left the offense in complete disarray.

Denver had to find a new starting quarterback, whether it meant promoting a backup, or signing a new starter. Being injured gave me time to observe both the defensive backs and quarterbacks. My main focus remained cornerback because I still had so much to learn, so I attended defensive back meetings only.

The Broncos paraded in one quarterback after another with no success. Tensi's backup from the previous year didn't deliver, so he was cut. The situation was dire entering the regular season.

And it got worse. The offense got nothing going. After releasing Tensi's backup from the previous year, Jim Leclair–a very nice guy, by the way–the Broncos pinned their hopes on a guy named Joe DiVito, who looked like the great Sonny Jurgensen. Joe had the same red hair and freckles, threw the same kind of ball and even had the stomach paunch. Everyone even called him "Sonny." But it was apparent Joe wasn't going to be the next Sonny Jurgensen on the field. All kidding aside, things weren't getting any better.

We opened with a 24-10 loss at Cincinnati, and then the bottom really started to fall out with a 34-2 loss at Kansas City.

The coaches, the team, the media and the fans were getting restless. Saban was desperate. I didn't read the papers back then, so unknown to me the media who had seen me play during the three-day camp were asking Saban about me. I didn't realize what was going on in that regard.

My leg was healing at that point, so it looked like I would be able to play the third week of the season at cornerback against the Boston Patriots, though not as the starter since I had been out five weeks. In those days, a player couldn't be cut when he was injured. When the player was healthy, he was either put back on the roster or cut. Some players would feign injury to stay on the injured list and not get cut so they could keep drawing a check–but that was not in my character. I would come back and either earn a check or move on. Once healthy, I expected to be cut even though I had been a starter. I thought the coaches might not have liked me because I had the clause for the three-day tryout.

I'd do my best to get well and let my ability determine what would happen next. I started running at full speed during the third week of the regular season. I went to practice ready to go and entered the locker room on a quiet day long before everyone else showed up. I looked in my locker and my heart sunk. My number 45 jersey was not hanging there. I saw number 15 in my locker. I thought they had cut me, signed a new quarterback and given him my locker.

"Oh, well," I said to myself, "my pro football career is over before it started. Maybe I'll be a school teacher."

I reached down and picked up my gear to put into my bag. It was time to clean out my locker, thank the Broncos for the chance, and get on with my life.

I saw the light flicker as someone entered the room. It was Lou Saban. He walked toward me. At least, I thought, he had the guts to give me my walking papers personally.

"Well, hello, my friend," Saban said. He always called people "my friend." That was the term he used for whatever reason, but I would never–especially in the year to come, consider him my friend. But in that moment, he sat down next to me.

"You see that number 15?" Saban asked.

"Yes, yes, I do, coach," I answered. "I guess you're replacing me with a quarterback since we need one."

"No, son," he said. "You are now a quarterback. We're going to give you a try."

At that point, my heart fell to my toes. I tried to show calm. But I was like a little kid. I was always wearing my game face, kind of a scowling demeanor. I could not help but grin. It was hard for me to maintain my composure.

"You don't mean that, do you?" I asked him.

"Yes, I do," Saban said. "We've been having a lot of problems at quarterback. We haven't been doing well. Here's your playbook. You're now a quarterback. Let's get busy."

My life changed at that point. Granted, at that point I was only supposed to be a backup. But I would, if it worked out, be a quarterback in professional football. I had a chance to be an African-American leader in what had been an all white institution.

When the press and my teammates found out I was going to get an opportunity to play the position I coveted, there was a lot of mixed reaction. The press gave me a lot of fanfare, since it was potentially a historical moment. It didn't dawn on me, the magnitude of what could possibly happen. I didn't realize I could be on my way to a place in history. I only wanted to be the best quarterback I could to help my team win.

I knew there would be some concerns among my teammates, or so I thought. African-Americans were still in the minority in pro sports, and that was the case on the Broncos.

For that third game–Boston Patriots, which is, of course, now New England–I was just the backup. As such, the reality was I didn't expect to play. In fact, I fully expected to be the backup until Steve Tensi got back, at which point I expected to be moved back to cornerback, or even cut.

Because he either wanted to limit my chances or just keep it simple for me, Saban gave me only a few plays so I wouldn't feel overloaded. Really, it still wasn't expected that I'd play. But even the backup had to know the offense just in case something happened.

Against Boston, I sat and watched the game. We were getting thoroughly beat in the first half. Our quarterback was non-productive, just getting no results. So in the fourth quarter, we were down, 20-7. I was told to go into the game.

"OK, Briscoe," Saban said, "get ready."

My heart started palpitating. I threw a few balls so hard the guy warming me up just looked at me. I was pumped. Eric Crabtree, a receiver on the team, had worked with me a lot during the tryouts and during practice when I was playing defense. Al Denson also came over to make sure I was calmed down.

I did the best to maintain the same demeanor I always had. My teammates were more excited than I was. My focus was to perform the best I could since there were only 10 minutes left in the game. No one expected much from me. I could let it all hang out. Since we were behind, there was no sense running the ball. I completed my first three passes. I scrambled a couple of times and got the ball down to the 12-yard line. I scrambled again and scored a touchdown. We got the ball again, moved down the field, and kicked a field goal, losing the game just 20-17.

The fans were going crazy, as were my teammates. I was out there playing sandlot football, basically, because I had only 10 plays, so I'd improvise and scramble and provide leadership. We got the ball and moved it, but time ran out and we lost 20-17. The fans were still excited, and my teammates were so happy.

Even the opposing team, Nick Buoniconti, a linebacker for the Patriots who would later become a friend and teammate in Miami, came over and congratulated me, telling me how they hadn't played against a quarterback who could run and throw like that. That day was another rite of passage for me as a 22-year-old man.

The media became a feeding frenzy after that. History would be made as I was slated to be the first black quarterback to start a game.

Though I was on the verge of realizing my dream, I had never thought about making history as the first black quarterback.

We would put together four wins in the next five games.

Heading into that first start, again, my first thoughts were about my teammates. There was a ton of attention—nonstop. But it all didn't affect them negatively one bit. I had earned respect from the time I came to Denver because of my work ethic and demeanor. Several of my teammates—especially the receivers—had been in camp for the three-day tryout, and I had developed a rapport with those guys. If there were any ill feelings from my teammates, I never saw or felt it. They gave me a lot of support

I was inundated throughout the week by the press for a lot of interviews. The press had a field day with my nickname from college, "Marlin the Magician."

The word spread around Denver. As I said before, Denver was a very racially tolerant city and had the reputation for being that way. There was no uproar or fervor from the fan base about having a black quarterback–at least not to my knowledge. I received a lot of support in terms of letters and contact from the public and press.

The attention quickly became national. All of the sudden, my starting at quarterback for the Broncos that week was being hailed as a history-making event. A lot of the black players really rallied around me. Many hadn't seen a black quarterback before, and knew that blacks didn't get the chance–it wasn't exactly a secret.

The white players really supported me, too, some very outwardly. I was concerned about the ones who were quiet and seemed noncommittal. Soon, though, I found out that those white guys were only being professional, and would support me if I led the team well and continued to improve my play–they were behind me if I got the job done, regardless of the color of my skin.

My life was pandemonium. In the city of Denver, my college nickname was resurrected. A sort of legacy was in its infant status. Denver has always been very supportive of its sports teams. At the old Mile High Stadium in 1968, seating capacity was nowhere near the 77,000 that became the standard in later decades. Yet for my first start, Denver was anticipating 25,000 additional fans.

I had a very close friend on that team–several, in fact. But one who was really close. His name was Drake Garrett, a black guy from Detroit who played for Michigan State.

Drake and I were different but we made great roommates and friends. I was wound pretty tight. Drake taught me how to relax, and not be so uptight. I taught him, too, about being grounded. Drake's free spirit used to get him in trouble. So we balanced each other out very well, and stimulated a healthy growth in each other. We remain close friends to this day.

Drake was also with me during the most trying time in my

young career. The spotlight was shining bright on me. Right after I was named the starter, it was back to business. On Monday each week, we were paid. We'd go back to practice on Tuesday.

I sensed that Saban wasn't too happy naming me the starter. Now, I have to make a statement here: My thoughts on the whole situation in regard to Lou Saban are my own. He is well thought of by a great majority of players who played for him throughout his career, black and white. I wasn't in that group. I thought he was overrated as a coach, and his career mark of 97-101-7, to me, is unremarkable. Just by his tone, and something that happened at the end of the 1968 season, led me to believe that Saban didn't want me, a black, quarterbacking his team. Saban never said as much, but that was my own, personal perception.

So back to the week of the Cincinnati game. The whirlwind week began with me being named the starter, and I believe it pained Saban to do that, from his tone to his body language. After all, he probably had to answer questions why he hadn't given me a chance after I stood out in the three-day tryout. I was a last-gasp measure after every other avenue had been exhausted. The fans and media had, in effect, clamored for me to get a chance. So I was thrust into that opportunity by default, in my view. That's why I question Saban's motivation and intention. Looking back, I don't know why Saban didn't give me more plays—and thus more chances—to be successful. I had run a full game plan in college and been very successful. I know the argument could be made that by limiting my plays, he was limiting my chances for failure, especially by being overloaded. I believe that down deep, he wanted me to fail so he could have Steve Tensi or someone else become his quarterback. I think he had no belief whatsoever that I could be a starting quarterback for his football team, and I believe his actions heading into the next season bore that point of view out very clearly. I think he hoped that I'd fail and move on, so he could move on. If that was his philosophy—and again, that's just my opinion—it would backfire on him.

8

Bogus Arrest Threatens Path

An unfortunate circumstance almost let Saban off the hook. That Monday, Drake and I picked up our checks. We went to a car dealership. I had ordered a new car for the first time in my life, a 1969 Riviera. It didn't cost a lot of money. My initial contract was $15,000, with a $6,000 signing bonus. That was quite a coup for a kid out of the Omaha projects. Teachers in those days made about $7,000 a year. So $15,000 for six months work doing something I loved seemed like a fortune. It's nowhere near what the young men playing pro football are making today, but you play the cards you are dealt in life.

On the way back from doing the paperwork for the car, we stopped at a department store. The ugly face of racism and prejudice were about to lock me in their crosshairs.

We went in to buy some records. Drake and I loved music. We also loved to party, and music was a part of that. We also had a little money. I didn't think about the dangers and potential problems. I purchased three record albums. Unfortunately, we were in an area of Denver that was predominantly white, a newly developed area.

The people in that store obviously weren't used to seeing two young black men in brand new leather coats. They had no idea who we were. I bought the album. The lady asked me for my receipts from the three albums I had bought earlier.

"But I bought all of these from you—not even an hour ago," I said, puzzled.

She asked again, so I pulled out a receipt and showed her.

"Where are the receipts for the other two?" she asked.

I pulled out another receipt.

"OK, where's the other receipt?" she asked.

I looked in my pockets and glanced in the bag. I had already opened the other album since I had bought it almost an hour earlier. It was Wes Montgomery's *Bumping on the Sunset.* But the receipt wasn't in the bag. I searched my pockets, but no luck.

And to be honest, it hadn't dawned on me to log and organize my receipts because I had done nothing wrong. I had paid for all three albums. The lady just rolled her eyes at me and I thought that was it.

Drake then paid for his albums. As we started to walk out, a security guard stopped us before we got out the door.

"I heard you can't find your receipt," a security guard said. "So you're going to be detained for shoplifting."

"I have the receipts," I said.

"No, I just saw you, and you produced two, not three," the guard said. "And you have three albums."

I reached into my pocket to look again. I couldn't find a receipt, but I did have $1,200 in cash. I held the money up to the guard.

"Why would I shoplift a record with this kind of money?" I asked. "You guys ask me for receipts, and I produce one. You ask me for another, I found that. I can't find one out of three—and I'm up there paying for another record—and you're saying that I shoplifted one."

The guard said, "Yes, that's right, and we're going to detain you."

He directed me to the back of the store. At that point, it wasn't that big of a deal. Drake told the guy again and again that he had seen me pay, that he witnessed it, and he named the album in the bag, and what it cost.

"This is ridiculous," Drake said. "The guy showed you two receipts. We've been walking around—and spending a lot of money in here. We'll find it if you give us a moment. If not, we'll pay for it—again."

But voices weren't raised or anything, and people were calm. I was especially calm because I knew I hadn't done anything wrong.

"What's your name?" the guard asked.

"Marlin Briscoe," I answered. "I can show you my driver's license."

"No, just sit here," he said.

He told Drake to leave, and then 10 minutes later he came back in the room.

"You are the quarterback for the Denver Broncos we've all been hearing about today?" he asked.

"Yes, I am," I answered, confused why that meant anything.

He put handcuffs on me. "We're going to have to arrest you," he said. "That's too bad you're the quarterback for the Broncos. We're taking you down, Briscoe."

"Why?" I asked.

Instead of walking me quietly through the back door where no one was, they paraded me out through the store in handcuffs, pointing out they had just arrested "the quarterback for the Denver Broncos." Everyone watched, and the white guard made a big deal out of how he was "taking down the quarterback for the Denver Broncos."

It was the most embarrassing thing that happened to me. And they let Drake take my records home! Even the one I supposedly shoplifted! I was mystified: How could they plan to charge me with shoplifting and let Drake take my records if they were stolen?

I called my cousin, Bob Rose, who had moved to Denver. He got me an attorney, and they got me out of jail.

At the police station, I talked to the officers and asked them to keep it out of the news.

"It's a misunderstanding," I pleaded. "I promise you, I will be quickly cleared. Please don't call the media until tomorrow because I know I can prove I bought that record."

"No problem," the officer told me. "We don't work that way."

Little did I know that by that time, the calls to the press had already been made and the story had already made the evening news.

So even before I got home, the story was on the news.

I called my mother. Sure enough the story had already broken back there.

"I assure you, Mom, I haven't done a thing," I told her. She was crying.

I would hear comments to the effect that "you can take the boy out of the projects, but you can't take the projects out of the boy." That stuff really got to me. What I got out of the projects was love, support and personal development. I wanted that stuff to stay with me.

Something else happened that evening. I sat down and talked to Drake about what had happened. He said he remembered me paying, even the change I got from the bill. So I felt vindicated in that regard.

Then, I sat down and took out the records that had caused me so much grief. If I was going to have my reputation smeared by *Bumping in the Sunset*, then I was going to at least enjoy it. I reached in to pull out the album.

And out from the album jacket came the receipt.

"Here it is! I knew I had it!" I said.

I called Bob and my attorney the next day. We had the whole thing straightened out in the matter of a couple of hours, producing the three receipts for the records. The timeline lined up just as Drake and I had said.

Yet it was all over the newspapers the next day, from Denver to Omaha and likely, points beyond. Actually, I knew the story made it nationwide because I'd hear about it again and again over the days, weeks and years to follow as I met people from other states who had read about it.

Ironically, what was front-page news—"Broncos quarterback arrested for shoplifting"—didn't make the front page the next day when I was vindicated. Charges were never even filed. Remember, I did nothing wrong!

I saw Coach Saban that morning, and he was concerned.

"What happened?" he asked.

"Coach, it's already been resolved," I said. "I had the receipts for all three records, and produced two of them at the store. After they paraded me around in handcuffs and took me to jail, I found the receipt right after I got out. The whole thing is done."

Saban said he believed me—which was good, because that was the truth—and the matter was dropped.

I heard—in 1999, in fact—that I had been suspended for the next game. Not true. I heard that I was charged with stealing. Not true.

Publicly, I never felt like my good name was cleared. My reputation was besmirched forever in some corners, and while I have certainly moved past it, I've never gotten past the way the media handled the follow-up story, which was treated as a brief, or non-story.

How can it be front-page news when I was arrested, and then moved back four pages when I was cleared? I felt like the coverage was race related. "Hoodlum quarterback arrested" was a whole lot sexier headline than "Quarterback cleared in misunderstanding."

That was the biggest public slap that I'd ever felt from the disgusting hand of racism because I believe in my heart that a white athlete would have gotten a fair shake, especially if he had a legitimate claim to his innocence—as I certainly had.

After talking to Coach Saban, I talked to my teammates, who were also concerned. That ended up not being a big deal because I found out my teammates knew me a lot better than I thought, knew the kind of person I was and the character I had. They knew stealing wasn't part of my character.

After the way the arrest and subsequent resolution were handled, I really developed a distrust of people. That wasn't how I was before it. Being from the Midwest, I had been very trusting. I quickly put up a wall and was much more guarded about what I said and whom I said it to.

I also had to get ready for Cincinnati. Anyone who follows football knows that a quarterback's toughest game is his second one. For his first appearance, the team doesn't have film to study on him, learn his characteristics, or find his weaknesses to exploit.

The Bengals did their homework on me, breaking down the film from the New England game. That led to a sub-par performance by me in that game. I don't know if the events of everything happening off the field had an effect, but that is possible. I certainly didn't play as well as I had hoped.

Steve Tensi came in for the second half because we were losing. He played great, and we won, 10-7. Steve got his position as starter back, as he deserved to. I had no problem with that, and it took a lot of the spotlight off me, and that was a nice break after the chaos from the week before.

Playing behind Steve really helped me learn. Steve was one of my staunchest supporters, then and now. We called him "Elvis" because he had those sideburns and a ducktail. He even played a guitar and sang Elvis songs. His white shoes were priceless. The guy really took me under his wing.

"Hey, forget about all of that negative publicity," Tensi said. "Everyone who matters knows you didn't do it—you couldn't have done it."

Playing the Jets and their star quarterback, Broadway Joe Namath, was almost surreal. There we were suddenly, in the center of the football universe in terms of attention as the Jets would go on to win the Super Bowl that season, beating the heavily favored Baltimore Colts and establishing Joe Namath as part of Americana.

Namath gave me a compliment after the game, and to this day whenever he sees me, he says, "There's the quarterback." That means so much, to be acknowledged by one of the game's greats, and one of the first, lasting stars of professional football's modern era. Joe always seats me at the quarterback's table when we attend the same function. I take a lot of pride in that. To be recognized by someone of his stature for what I did in just one year at quarterback means more than I could ever express in mere words. We beat the Jets 21-13.

After playing the Jets, we headed to San Diego for Game six. The Chargers had John Hadl, Speedy Duncan, Dickey Post and the legendary Lance Alworth, who would become a key in my life more than a decade later.

We went to San Diego, and I picked up a newspaper before the game. A writer called me "Mandrake the Magician." That's how much of a joke they thought I was.

They didn't feel that way for long.

I threw three touchdown passes and ran for another as we lost 55-24. If our defense hadn't given up a lot of yards and points, we would have won. The Chargers did have a plethora of offensive weapons back then, and were hard to stop. The same sportswriter did get my name right after that game.

I had a big game the next week against the up-and-coming Miami Dolphins. Down 14 points in the third quarter, we came back as I ran in 10 yards on a quarterback sneak to give us the win, 21-14, capping a 21-0 rally for us.

"Marlin subbed superbly for Steve Tensi, and rallied the Broncos from a 14-point third-quarter deficit," says the long-time voice of the Broncos, the late Bob Martin, on the Broncos' season recap video. "Marlin displayed the ability to roll out and scramble. He brought additional excitement to the Bronco's attack. With time running out and a tie imminent, Marlin drove the Broncos steadily down the field. With less than two minutes left, he stunned everyone with a daring quarterback sneak from 10 yards out and won the game."

Then, we avenged the earlier loss to the Patriots at Boston's Fenway Park, with a 35-14 win on the road. Our record was 4-4 as Tensi returned to the lineup, solidly completing 11-of-17 passes.

We prepared to play the Oakland Raiders the next week. They had one of the fiercest teams in the league. That was our first of two games against them that year, as teams play each team in their division twice.

The Raiders had a player named Eldridge Dickey, who was being groomed to be the first black quarterback after a successful college career at quarterback for Tennessee State. The Raiders had drafted him in the first round of the 1968 draft.

So he was clearly supposed to make history, not me.

Dickey had come into camp that year as a rookie and had given the veteran quarterbacks a good run for the starting job—the way the story was told to me was that Dickey had performed better in camp than Ken Stabler. What I was told is that Al Davis had drafted Dickey especially to make him the first black quarterback. That's who Al Davis is—he likes to be the first and win at everything, whether it's something that's worth battling for, or not.

The story went that Dickey was told that if he would move to receiver, that he'd be the first black quarterback eventually, and he got a little more money to acquiesce. Apparently he did.

The way events unfolded in Denver that year wrecked the plans to make Dickey the first black to start at quarterback. There's no doubt in my mind that he was earmarked to be drafted out of college and become pro football's first black starting quarterback. I just happened to get there before he did.

When the Raiders came to Denver to play us, Dickey came to my apartment. He was very cordial when he was introduced to me.

He was gracious and congratulated me on breaking that color barrier. I could tell by his body language that he was disappointed I had leapfrogged ahead of him. But I give the guy credit because he had the dignity and class to wish me nothing but the best. Clearly, he coveted that historical moment that had been wrested from him. But that's just the way the chips fell. And people move on.

Steve Tensi started against the Raiders. Oakland wasn't a group of dummies. They knew he was immobile and coming off an injury. The Raiders blitzed him relentlessly. Finally, they got him really hard, busting up his shoulder. Because of this unfortunate circumstance, I was installed as the starting quarterback for the Denver Broncos the rest of the year after that 43-7 loss to Oakland.

Becoming the starter ensured my official place in history. I wasn't a one-game starter who would be cast to the side. I'd have the rest of the season to start at quarterback. I was to lead my team the rest of the season. It was a situation I was thrust into that had a huge responsibility. The media poured back in. I was asked time and time again about the shoplifting incident, as many in the media from outside the city had never heard that not only was I not charged, but completely cleared.

Since I had that break leading up to the Raiders game, my head had a chance to clear. When I was named the starter for the rest of the season, I had to think to myself: What kind of precedent will I set for black quarterbacks in America if I fail? This was the last position that blacks had not gotten a chance at—for racist reasons, in my view. The attitude was a black man couldn't think deep enough to be quarterback, couldn't throw well enough, and couldn't lead a team.

If I succeeded or failed—and I hate that word, fail—it would cement people's perceptions, one way or another, about a black man's capability of playing quarterback. I knew I was championing a cause. Coverage would not just review me, but indeed those reviews would be applied to all aspiring black quarterbacks. I thought, "If I make it, they will have hope." It really dawned on me that I was carrying a torch for a huge group.

Ebony magazine came out to do a story on me.

Saban told the magazine, "He's got a lot to learn, but he's receptive and he knows he's got a lot to learn. That's the most important thing." He added that my best traits were my "ability to run, good instincts and throwing ability." Saban went on to say that leadership was very important, and that with me, "there was no question there. He's got stuff." Of course, even though I did nothing from that point forward but set records and improve, Saban would never again let onto what he thought my abilities were, or were not.

Tensi provided Ebony with this comment: "He's a hell of a ball player. What he lacks in experience, he makes up in talent. It takes a lot of pressure off me, having a guy like that behind me." It doesn't take a rocket scientist to figure out that Steve Tensi figured I'd be back the next year to back him up when he was healthy. I know that's what I was assuming if things worked out right.

The support of Tensi, my teammates and my belief in myself left me extremely confident. I knew I had the mental and physical ability to succeed, regardless of my color.

Though Saban to this day cites my size as the reason I wouldn't make it as a quarterback, I never viewed that as a valid point. My size never held me back in anything, football or basketball. A quarterback would have to be at least 7-feet tall to see clearly over the offensive line. Quarterbacks now are regularly at or shortly below 6-feet tall, and Doug Flutie isn't as tall as I am, yet look at the career that man has put up.

Quarterbacks throw through passing alleys. You will almost never see quarterbacks drop back and regularly throw over the heads of linemen who are standing up, blocking. Even if that were possible, they couldn't throw over the heads and outstretched arms of rushing defenders. Thus, quarterbacks look for passing alleys.

Denver was not the major media center back then that it is today, and the Broncos didn't have the national following that they do today. The AFL teams like the Raiders, Jets and Chiefs—and occasionally the Chargers—got the bulk of national attention.

Anyway, after the loss to Oakland, we fell to Houston, 38-17, on the road. Buffalo came to Denver the next week.

When we played the Bills, we had a strange occurrence. Floyd Little, the great running back who wore No. 44 and would go on to make the Denver Broncos Ring of Fame, was falling out of favor with Saban. Floyd had fumbled the ball late in the game when all we had to do was run the clock out. Buffalo took it deep into our territory and made the go-ahead field goal taking a 32-31 lead. We went to the sidelines and Saban let Floyd have it.

"You're cut!" Saban yelled to Little, telling him he was benched.

He sent Fran Lynch into the game. Fran was a good back—and a real hard runner—but he was no Floyd Little. Fran came into the game, and I was trying to figure out what to do because we needed Floyd and his speed for the play we were going to run. Saban was screaming. The play we were going to run involved sending a running back out on a deep pattern with a linebacker covering him. All of the sudden, Floyd came running to the huddle. We all looked at him confused.

"Lou sent me in," Floyd said, though that hadn't been the case. "Throw the ball as far as you can, Marlin. I'll be there."

Fran went to the sidelines. I ran out of the pocket to the left side on the play and hit Floyd with a long pass—on the season highlight film, you can clearly see that I throw the ball at our 27-yard line near the left sideline, and Floyd catches it near the right sideline on the Buffalo 18-yard line. The ball traveled 55 yards in the air, and at least 20 yards across the field—from the numeral on the left side of the field to the numeral on the right—and Floyd dove, making a great catch. That set up the game-winning field goal. I had three touchdown passes that game and we pulled out a 34-32 win.

Each day I was improving as a quarterback. I learned both the cerebral part of the game and how to fuse it with my athletic ability, throwing and leadership. We started playing some good football.

I had another three-touchdown game against San Diego at Mile High Stadium in Denver, though the defense struggled—Lance Alworth had three touchdowns 25 minutes into the game—and we lost 47-23. Even though we rallied passing the ball, it was too much of a hole to dig out of against San Diego.

And then we went to Oakland, where it was time to bring a part of my past into my present.

Earlier, I wrote about how I moved to Omaha when I was young. We moved there from Oakland. My father, to the best of my knowledge, was still there. My mom had never said a bad word about him, and I really had no ill feelings toward him. He just wasn't there. But when we headed to Oakland and got to the hotel, I had a phone call.

That was a bittersweet occasion. I had no idea I would meet up with him or anything. He did call my sister and me during the holidays and tried to send a little money here and there. Still, I had no memory of ever meeting this man who had the same name, Marlin Briscoe. I was "Junior."

As it turned out, my father was very proud of me, bragging, "That's my boy." The little boy who was out of his life was now a man. When we got to the hotel, it was Saturday. Drake and I decided to go see the sights. As we prepared to leave the hotel, the phone rang. On the other end of the line was a voice I remembered from phone calls on Christmas when I was a kid.

"I'd like to come over, and take you out," he said.

I said that would be fine. I didn't have any animosity. And I have to admit that in the back of my mind, I thought I might get a chance to meet him again at some point. I was so curious to see him. I had asked my mother about my dad, mostly things like how tall he was. She said he was only 5-foot-3. Sure enough, he shows up in this little hat, and he really was 5-3. He looked just as he had in the pictures my mother had showed us. I could tell by his build and his face that he was where I came from. He took me to his neighborhood, showing me where I had lived.

We just kind of looked at each other at first. I hadn't seen him since I was a baby, so I had no real memory of him. He took me to the pool hall to meet his friends, and brag to them about me. I learned a lot about him. He was a World War II veteran and worked for the government. I never got involved in what had happened between him and my mother. She had chosen to take the high road and so did he, and I appreciated not being put in the middle at any time in my life.

I was proud to see he was a well-dressed man and very articulate. He drove a Ford Thunderbird. We had the same taste in just about everything, and we both even liked to shoot pool. We hung out, but I had a curfew and had to be back for dinner. But I enjoyed meeting my father for the first time. When we got back to the hotel, I got him some tickets for the game. Thank God for that visit, because, as I will explain in further detail later, I lost contact with my father years later when I fell into drugs.

Meeting him must have inspired me. I came out on fire. The

Raiders had seen me when I replaced Tensi, but I wasn't great that first time. I threw three touchdown passes in the first half as we rallied from behind for a 20-10 lead.

We got greedy, though. On the last play of the first half, I was going for the big one. I threw a bomb and was knocked out by Ben Davidson. I was all groggy for the second half, and we lost 33-27.

Still that game was progress. To throw that many TD passes against the Raiders, a much superior team than the Chargers, really sealed my ascension to respectability in the league. The Raiders had seen plenty of film on me, and I was still able to tear them up in the first half. The word was finally getting out that the Denver Broncos weren't an easy game anymore; however, Kansas City waxed us in the season finale. I probably shouldn't have played after the concussion that I suffered the previous week, but I wasn't about to let my teammates down when we had to pull together more than ever.

We had our problems, but we were one very entertaining team, we playing with a lot of excitement. We gave up a lot of points—remember, we had an all rookie secondary, and I'd have been one of those guys if I hadn't been moved to quarterback.

Despite my not playing quarterback, and thus having no effect on our first two games of the season—both were horrible offensive performances and losses—we still ranked 16th out of 26 teams in the league in points scored, and remember that our defense finished second to the last in the league in points allowed, as our opponents scored 404 points on us. Our record was 5-9. Our defense gave up at least 30 points in each of the final six games of the season—and twice in that span it yielded more than 40.

We tailed off sharply to end the season, though we did put up a total of 50 points in losses to San Diego and the Raiders, our defense gave up 80 points in those two contests. So we ended the season on a three-game losing streak despite producing some very impressive offensive outings.

I ended up throwing for 1,589 yards and 14 touchdown passes in the seven games I started and the four others I got into—a rookie record for touchdown passes that still stands for the Denver Broncos. I also rushed for 308 yards, giving me 1,897 yards of total offense—also a rookie record for Denver, ahead of Mickey Slaughter and John Elway. My average gain per offensive play of 7.16 yards is still third best among Bronco players—not just rookies—and is just .14 behind being the team's all-time leader in that category. The 333 yards of total offense I had against Buffalo is second all-time best among Broncos rookies, with Elway first at 368 yards of total offense against the then-Baltimore Colts.

Joe Namath threw only 15 touchdown passes his rookie year, playing a lot more in his rookie season than I did, and Joe had been named rookie of the year two years earlier.

But I did finish second—runner-up—for rookie of the year. Paul Robinson, a running back for Cincinnati, who ran for more than 1,000 yards and started all year, and won rookie of the year.

I was honored. It was a real boost, and it solidified my standing as a quarterback, that I not only played, but also played well enough to be recognized.

Say this or that, that I'm too short or whatever, but the numbers don't lie. Those numbers prove a black man can think, throw and lead a team.

All and all, despite the problems—the arrest, and not starting the year at quarterback—it was a good year. And getting arrested was a good lesson on how careful a young black professional athlete had to be, from who he associated with to the restaurants and stores that he frequented. I had developed a whole new set of responsibilities.

Right before the 1968 season ended, my college sweetheart, Beverly Wright, came to visit. I should have married her. We did plan on getting married. Because of my newfound fame, I put it off. I wasn't mature enough to accept the fact that I had found the right person. I was 22, and I let the best opportunity in the world pass me by in not marrying her. To this day, I call that one of the worst decisions of my life.

After the season ended, I was thinking that I had finally proved to the world that its ideas about black quarterbacks were wrong. I relished the challenge of facing Steve Tensi for the position the next season.

I toyed with the idea of staying in Denver and playing in the American Basketball Association for the Denver Rockets. I held my own playing ball against guys from the Rockets when we played pick-up games. A lot of people really pushed me to become a two-sport professional athlete.

Something more pressing was calling: my education. I had made a commitment to get my degree, and because of changing majors, I was six hours short. Education was why I went to college in the first place. On top of that, I had promised my mother I would graduate. Though I did have a good rookie year for Denver, I was only two years removed from a broken neck that had taught me that sports could end on the next play.

That hamstring injury from my first year reminded me that I needed something to fall back on. I saw great players hanging on, who were over the hill or playing through injuries that would wreck their bodies in the years to come. But they had nothing to fall back on. Football was their lives. It was heartbreaking to see these one-time warriors limp to keep a paycheck. On occasion, I saw these grown men cry, and that only reaffirmed my commitment to graduate.

I arrived home in Omaha to a hero's welcome from all the people I had grown up with, gone to high school and college with. A lot of them had visited me at my apartment in Denver, and I had taken them around town. They threw me a party when I got back home to Omaha. I got my feet back on the ground, and that perspective was great. I played some basketball to stay in shape and worked out hard for football. I tried to mend fences with Beverly, but we fell farther and farther apart. I remain friends with that wonderful lady to this day.

I went back to Omaha University, which had just joined the University of Nebraska system to get state funds, and was renamed the University of Nebraska-Omaha. I worked through the schooling and made plans to student teach to finish up the requirements for my degree.

9

Conspiracy Derails Denver Journey

An interesting call came one day from a teammate back in Denver. A conspiracy to get me out of the quarterback picture was underway. I had heard through the newspaper that Pete Liske, a good quarterback in the Canadian Football League, had been signed by Denver to compete for a job. I didn't really give that a second thought. I thought I had proven myself, so I welcomed the competition. I never asked to be handed the job, only to be able to compete.

My teammate told me that quarterback meetings were quietly being held.

Yet I was never invited.

How fair was that? If you're only as a good as your last game, how could I be excluded? How could this not be race related? Based on what I had done—rookie of the year runner-up, a rookie club record 14 touchdown passes—I had earned a shot to compete for a position.

Quickly, I had to come up with a plan to stave off whatever Lou Saban was planning to do to get me out of the picture in Denver.

But I had to do it with dignity and pride. Hearing news of these surreptitious meetings of the minds gave me the idea of making an unannounced trip to Denver to see what was going on. I received my degree, and immediately caught a flight to Denver. Another teammate told me when these meetings were being held.

I showed up on time, and you should have seen the look of surprise on certain faces when I walked in the door. Pete Liske, Steve Tensi and Lou Saban were in a meeting when I got there. I just waited around, much to the chagrin of people who knew what was going on. I just sat and waited

Within an hour, out of the door come Pete, Steve and Coach Saban, carrying playbooks. Pete didn't know me, but Saban and Steve looked like they had seen a ghost. Steve, who was a mentor and friend, looked at me and bowed his head. It wasn't his doing, and he couldn't jeopardize his job for me. Saban looked at me like, "So what?" He literally did not say a word to me, no explanation, no greeting—nothing. He just brushed right past me.

After Saban was gone, Steve came to talk to me. He did his best to console me. He saw the look of hurt in my eyes, and the pain in my body language.

"Marlin, I am so sorry," Steve said. He didn't even need to say that—this was not his doing, it was Saban. Steve was trying to make a living and was coming off a pretty serious injury, so he had himself, his family and his career to think about. This was all done in management, and that was Saban, who was in complete control.

I couldn't believe Saban had completely ignored me. But I kept my calm. I took it for what it was—another fork in the road, another challenge. My thought process was pretty simple because I didn't have any real options. I knew at that point that I wouldn't get a chance in Denver. Saban would have to publicly let me play quarterback in camp before deciding Steve and Pete were his quarterbacks—something he had clearly already decided.

The media and fans—and everyone else within Denver's football community—knew what I had done the previous year. In the weeks that followed, the media had a lot of stories about the quarterback competition. If only they knew that there would be no competition based on who was invited to the clandestine quarterback camp. If Saban truly believed I was too small to be his quarterback—something he would say years later—then I might've believed that was how he really felt. If he would have told me that, then I could have prepared to play defensive back or whatever. But he didn't.

He never told me a word that I was too small or anything

else—he never told me anything, period. That's why I believe—and always will—that it was racial, that he simply wouldn't have a black quarterback. Now, let me be clear: Saban could probably line up a hundred black players from other positions who had good careers for him, and they would say he was not a racist in any way whatsoever. And I'm not saying he was a racist. But it will always be my belief that he did not want me to be his quarterback for the simple reason that I was black. He didn't invite me to those quarterback meetings and didn't give me any reason. He had every chance when the season ended and another chance that day when I showed up and saw him, Steve and Pete. However, he didn't. He could have told me at season's end that I wouldn't be able to compete at quarterback—or even told me to prepare to go back to defensive back. He never said a word either way. So I assumed I'd compete for the quarterback job. And I thought it was fair to believe that since I had done such a decent job as a rookie, that I'd have a chance to compete to back up Tensi.

I never did let on publicly about what had happened with those meetings. I knew I had only one route, and that was to keep moving forward. I didn't want to go to the media because I didn't want a spectacle or controversy. That would have been counterproductive to the team goals we had for the season. I rolled up my sleeves and decided to compete. I stayed in Denver from that point and worked out.

From the first practice, it was obvious from the beginning that I wasn't going to be considered a candidate by the way Saban handled things. He ignored me more than I thought was humanly possible during the training camp sessions, not even acknowledging my presence. So it was clear that he would go with Steve and Pete.

What I did have a problem with is he didn't let me compete. I could have raised the level of competition. He made it difficult for me in training camp, physically and mentally. I was third in line at the opening of training camp. Obviously, this was to be the trend.

I grew increasingly frustrated. I didn't want to create a racial situation publicly. I had heard some other teams were interested in me. Apparently, they had heard that Saban had no real plans for letting me compete for the quarterback position. Based on that information I thought it was, perhaps, time to move on. I asked Saban if

I could come by his office because I didn't want anyone to know that I was asking for my release.

Saban must've really wanted to cut me on his own terms because I knew at the time that other teams in the league looking for quarterbacks were inquiring if I would be available since. I heard that Hank Stram told several of his players that he wanted to bring me to Kansas City and work on an offense with a moving pocket.

I was cordial to Saban. I knew this man was not my ally, but I wanted to keep from making an enemy. I wasn't upset. I knew how to negotiate, which meant remaining calm. In addition, the simple, plain truth was that players had no strength in those days in terms of bargaining power.

"Coach, I sense that my days here might be numbered, so I'd like to ask for my release," I said. "Thanks for last season."

Saban never looked me in the eye. For the first time I saw embarrassment in his face and eyes. He didn't say a word. He looked away, as if in deep thought.

"Yes, I can do that," Saban said. "But can you wait four days? And can you keep this completely between us for now?"

I had no idea why he wanted to do it that way, but I said yes. I also had no doubt he wanted me to be gone. By asking for my release I thought I was taking pressure off him, and giving myself time to find another team since I had heard from players on at least four other teams that I would be signed immediately, even within hours upon being released.

I knew I needed to get my release, and Saban was in a position to demand any terms he wanted. Looking back, I wish I had done my homework and found out how releases and waiving players worked.

"We will make it public in four days," Saban said.

I was released four days later, with no fanfare.

And no takers.

No takers for the runner-up rookie of the year? Are you kidding me? I found it strange that no one would give me a tryout even, based on the feedback I had gotten from players on other teams that had heard my name several time from their coaches as a player they'd like to bring in.

I was confused, especially because I had really had a good training camp to that point. Then, it hit me: Saban could've said some-thing to people in the league, or had someone spread something around, calling me a malcontent or doing something to my reputa-tion. Those four days gave him plenty of time to make calls, or have someone else do his dirty work, to in effect blackball me. Giving him those four days was a huge mistake. These are my opinions only, and I had no evidence to pin that on him, especially in those days of the good ol' (white) boy network that was professional foot-ball.

In the long term, every team I played on would beat Saban-coached teams. He was one of the real nomads in the history of the sport. After leaving pro football with a sub-.500 career record, he landed at—of all places—Peru State, Nebraska, not that far from Omaha, for one season. Go figure.

Since I was not going to be in Denver—or anywhere else in pro football after I found no interest—I decided to go back to Omaha and make plans to go on about my life. I figured my football career was over.

I went back to Omaha and stayed with my mother. I always hoped some team would give me a call, so I worked out twice a day since training camps were still going on. I talked to former team-mates and coaches. Al Caniglia gave me the best advice, and he told me he had no doubts that I had been bad-mouthed and labeled a troublemaker.

"You belong in the league," Coach Al said. "You proved your-self. Someone will give you a shot. Keep working, and keep your head up."

I worked out at the college and threw with the kids at Omaha U., who were in the classes behind me. A week later, I went to one of my receivers and close childhood friends, Rick Davis, who has since died. He was full of confidence, really cocky. He had become a successful insurance agent. I was sitting in his office 10 days into my exile from Denver.

"Bris, Bris, we've played ball forever," he said. "You were a run-ning back in high school and could catch the ball. Why don't you try playing receiver?"

"Receiver?" I asked.

He made a motion with his hands as if he were catching a ball.

"You know, receiver," he said. "You're an athlete. It's obvious they won't let you play quarterback."

I don't know why he said receiver, since I had gone to Denver as a defensive back. But Rick had been a receiver, so he knew what he was talking about.

Then, I went to Ken Fischer who was my defensive coach at Omaha U.

"You should be a receiver," Ken said, without prompting. "You could do that in pro ball. I have no doubt."

Once again, I kind of laughed it off.

10

Fleeing to Canada, and then New Life in Buffalo

I decided to explore the waters of the Canadian Football League. The British Columbia Lions had selected me in their draft out of college. But I had chosen Denver. The CFL had more racial tolerance in terms of letting blacks play quarterback, something that would live on for decades. Warren Moon, one of the great passers in NFL history who was finally allowed to come back from the CFL and play quarterback in the NFL, could attest to the truth of that. Moon was big and strong-armed—why did it take so long for this college star to get his NFL break?

Anyway, I called British Columbia, and to my surprise, they offered me the chance to play quarterback and defensive back as well.

I had no other opportunities in the United States. So I thought I'd do what Pete Liske did—play well in Canada, and get back to the U.S.

So off I went to Vancouver. If the AFL paid peanuts, then the Canadian Football League paid peanut shells. But football was football, and the CFL was professional football. I took a flight to Canada and went to the practice site. I went to camp but hadn't signed a contract because I wanted to get a feel for what Canadian football was like before I was legally bound to a team. So I worked out with the B.C. Lions.

Being used to the American game, I didn't like the Canadian

game at first. It wasn't anything against the Canadians, or their league. The field was wide and the ball was bigger. Though the players worked hard, it was clear the game was not on as high a level as the AFL or NFL. Not to disparage the league, but I wasn't impressed. I felt like I had already excelled at a higher level, and that the CFL wasn't for me.

I also knew that if I wanted to stay in professional football, the CFL would probably have to be for me until I got back to where I could compete for a job in the AFL or NFL. The Canadian season had started, so I needed to sign the next day. They offered me a contract and had gotten me a uniform to get me ready to play that week as the CFL started a few weeks before the American pro leagues. In short, the B.C. Lions treated me very well.

So I went to the hotel where I was staying. I was doing flip-flops—should I stay or not? I was getting ready to sign and just make the best of it. I took a physical and was issued a playbook. I sat in my hotel and was reading the contract, pondering my future.

I had a lot of angst sitting there in the hotel room pondering my future.

"Is this it for me? Canadian football?" I asked myself.

I answered, "You can't let Lou Saban and what happened in Denver defeat you. That's what they've done. You've let them win. They've exiled you to Canada. You didn't put up a fight like you should have."

What I did next changed the course of my life and was the second-biggest decision I made besides that first three-day quarterback tryout my first year in Denver.

I got on the phone at the hotel that night and called as many teams as I could, mostly ones against whom I had experienced success my first year with Denver—the one thing I hadn't done when Saban took those four days to sully my negotiating position. My mistake was in waiting for them to call me.

I heard some interesting stories, but the important thing was they were still interested in me. I called the San Diego Chargers, the Kansas City Chiefs and the Buffalo Bills. The Bills said they were interested but didn't know where I was. Of course, they could have called Omaha University and tracked me down in a heartbeat. But the important thing was, they were interested. All of the teams said they were set at quarterback but they'd give me a shot at another position.

"We're looking at you as an athlete, not as a quarterback," Buffalo coach John Rauch said. "As a defensive back or as a wide receiver."

Rauch had been named the new head coach at Buffalo. He had coached the Raiders the previous year and I had put up big numbers against the Raiders in Oakland, so he knew I would compete.

"We're set at quarterback," Rauch said. "We drafted James Harris."

That right there said a lot about Rauch and the Bills. Harris was a highly regarded quarterback, and he was black. Of course, I had known they drafted James, and it was a great move. They already had several good quarterbacks, including Jack Kemp and Tom Flores—two of the men whom I respect the most in this world.

"But I do have an immediate problem that you could help out with, if you want," Rauch said.

"Sure, Coach, you name it," I said.

"All three of our quarterbacks are hurt now, and it's killing what we're trying to do in (training) camp," Rauch said. "Can you come in and be an emergency quarterback for us now? I don't want to disillusion you; the quarterback thing is just until our guys are healed. If you make this team, Marlin, it will be at receiver. We just need you to throw in practice and basically pick up the slack. I don't want to mislead you, Marlin, because we're set at quarterback. But there might be another place here for you as a receiver, especially."

I could tell Coach Rauch was excited to talk to me and that meant a lot. Buffalo had a number one receiver in Haven Moses, a high draft pick out of San Diego State. I didn't know of any of their other receivers, so I thought I might have a chance.

Still, I thought to myself, "Who I am kidding? I've never played receiver before."

But Buffalo had a revolving door trying to find someone who would complement Haven on the left side. Less than three weeks until the season started…

"I'll be there, Coach, tomorrow," I said.

"We'll be glad to have you, Marlin," Rauch said pleasantly. "I'll have the arrangements made for you to fly here. There will be a plane ticket waiting for you at the airport."

Even though I had confidence in my ability and was resilient, the odds, I felt, were stacked against me to make a team at a position I had never played before. I sat on my bed in Vancouver thinking, "This will be darn near impossible."

Even for someone who played receiver all his life, it would be tough to make a team in three weeks.

"I'm going back to the NFL," I said aloud in my empty hotel room. "I'm going to accept this challenge, and I'm going to fight my way back in."

That night, Coach Rauch sent me a ticket after we agreed to terms. I literally slipped out of the hotel room and didn't tell a soul. I'm not proud of that, but my mind was haywire.

It's no excuse that I was a 23-year-old confused young man. But I probably would have left in a week or two. Though I'd change it and have called them if I could do it over, I did what I had to do.

That meant going to Buffalo.

The best decision I ever made in my career was negotiating my own contract with the Broncos. If that hadn't happened, I wouldn't have been able to become the first regular black quarterback. The second best decision, though, was signing with Buffalo.

I flew from Vancouver to Buffalo and was met at the airport by Elbert Dubenion, Buffalo's chief scout who had been a great receiver for the Bills in the early 1960s. On the way out of the airport, he told me about their needs at receiver, and how I could best fit into the team.

When it comes right down to it, my signing was hardly even a footnote for Buffalo at the time because the big news was that Buffalo had drafted and signed O.J. Simpson out of the University of Southern California. Everything in Buffalo was "Juice this" or "Juice that." Though I hadn't yet met Simpson, I had followed his career in college because our careers overlapped, and we were in the same backfield on a post-season all-star list in 1967. He had received a lot of exposure and was widely regarded as the greatest college running back ever.

Dubenion checked me in at camp, and I met Coach Rauch, who was elated to see me—that made me feel great. Rauch talked at length about how well I had played last year, recapping the game for Dubenion. Rauch was sincere, and I could tell he liked—and respected—me. That was a huge change from what I had experienced with Lou Saban in Denver. In Rauch, I had a coach who really wanted to see me succeed. In fact, in order for the team to succeed, he needed me to reach my potential and fill the spot he had hoped me to fill—what a great feeling that was for me, especially since I was clearly in limbo as far as my chances of making the team. It took away quite a bit of the trepidation about learning a position that I had never played in my life—wide receiver.

There were just two preseason games left before the final cut. I had my work cut out for me, no question about that.

My first day at the Bills' camp, I was introduced to James Harris. He would go on to build the Baltimore Ravens into a Super Bowl winner in 2000 as the player personnel director—in a position most often held by whites. But the Ravens' franchise was so progressive in that regard that Harris was hired by another black, the great Cleveland tight end Ozzie Newsome.

Meeting Harris was great.

"I never thought I'd get to meet you," Harris said. "Especially not in a situation like this. I watched you last year. What you did was good—special. You, Marlin, were the reason I was drafted (in the eighth round) this year. What you did set the stage for other blacks. Now, we're on the same team!"

I was so proud that James shared that with me. That encounter sent me out to practice with a new vigor. We hit it off immediately. Obviously, we had a common bond. But he was also a great person.

James had a pulled groin and wasn't able to practice yet. So my first line of duty was quarterback. I quickly learned the playbook and was throwing in the first practice. All I really did the first few days was throw and learn the playbook. That was fun, and I felt like I excelled, but it was clearly setting me back as far as earning a spot by learning receiver.

Though I had played against—and beaten—Buffalo the previous year as Denver's quarterback, the 1969 Bills had a lot of new faces. The front office had signed a lot of younger guys because a good number of the previous year's team were older guys on the downside of their careers.

But Buffalo did have Haven Moses, and Wayne Patrick. All

three of the quarterbacks—Harris, Kemp and Flores—immediately embraced me. James and I would be close for years to come. But I also really enjoyed Jack Kemp and Flores.

Kemp carried himself with so much grace and poise and was a great leader. A lot of the Bills players told me, "Denver treated you like trash with what happened (in training camp)" and I certainly couldn't disagree with that. A lot of those guys, Kemp included, said they sympathized with me. I really felt like I was being taken into a family. Being told by so many people that they were glad to have me made me feel better. Keep in mind my mental state after experiences with Denver.

I was still just a stopgap at quarterback, though it felt good to play quarterback again. By the second day, I was really back in rhythm and was getting to know the receivers. Rauch had always run a pass-oriented offense with all the passing-game talent the Raiders had assimilated. This would lead to problems with O.J. in Buffalo that season. But the pre-season was a blast for me. I was able to throw the long ball—without anybody hustling me out of the drills.

After each practice I started working out as a receiver. It was taxing, but rewarding, and certainly challenging. Three days into practice, I was contemplating my chances of making the team. Buffalo had a lot of receivers. And though none had stepped up as a good weapon to free up Haven, these guys all still had NFL experience—and college—at receiver. I, on the other hand, had never run a route, and I wasn't as fast as most of the guys.

On that third day, I was feeling the pressure. O.J. was running a route in the flat. At the time, O.J. didn't have a helmet—his head was too big, literally, and the Bills had no helmet large enough for O.J.'s skull. Boy, the guys on the team—especially the veterans who hadn't yet grown fond of O.J.'s constant trash talking—had a field day with that.

So he went without (a helmet) while they sent for his college helmet from USC. O.J. was a very lackadaisical pass catcher because his forte was running the football. He wasn't thrilled with Rauch's passing philosophy.

I threw a pass to O.J., and he just let it go. All he had to do was reach for it. He started back toward the line of scrimmage.

"You aren't a quarterback, brother," O.J. said. "You're a wide receiver."

I couldn't believe he said that. Now, the truth of the matter is that O.J. was always talking, literally nonstop. And he probably didn't mean anything by it. Here he was, this big bonus baby, and he just wanted to deflect the blame for not catching the pass.

O.J.'s personality was that he'd say anything. Without thinking at all, he'd speak his mind. Some of us called him "motor mouth." He offended some people, but he really was harmless and loved the attention that the spotlight brought.

That didn't matter.

Something in my mind snapped. I had heard from Lou Saban that I was no quarterback. I had heard it from every other NFL and AFL team in the form of no phone calls when Saban released me. And now I was hearing it in Buffalo.

All the frustration bubbled to the surface.

I picked up a football, and fired it at O.J. I mean, I threw a rocket. He moved just in time so that the ball missed his head and bounced off his shoulder pads.

Silence fell over camp. No one moved.

Certainly, no one could believe that the new guy—the cast-off, if you will—had thrown a $10 football at the top draft pick's uncovered head.

At that point, I was pretty much expecting a plane ticket and my walking papers. O.J. didn't say a word to me, but asked the player closest to him, "Why is this brother throwing a ball at me?"

Something strange happened in that moment: I had earned the respect of the entire Buffalo Bills team. I became a leader with a very thoughtless, emotional reaction.

We went on with the drills. None of the coaches or players said a word. We went back to work, and had a very professional, efficient practice.

James Harris came over when practice ended.

"Don't take what Juice said seriously," Harris said. "He just talks."

"It's cool," I said. Harris smiled widely.

Then, someone else came up to me: O.J.

"Sorry, for what I said," O.J. said. "That wasn't cool."

I nodded that things were fine, and actually apologized for zinging that ball at his head. Simpson simply had no idea of the hurt that had been inside me since I found I wouldn't be competing for the quarterback job in Denver. O.J. and some of the other guys really started hanging out with me at that point.

That whole crazy—actually silly—incident sparked an aura of respect around me, simply for taking a high-profile rookie to task for mouthing off. The veterans approved because they had wanted to shut up O.J. The other rookies liked me, probably because O.J.'s star stature spawned a huge shadow and kept them out of the spotlight. And like I said, from that moment on, O.J. was very good to me.

So everyone on the team made it known from that moment on that I was welcome. The coaches never said anything, but I truly believe after giving it some thought that they respected me for setting a tone for that team. No one really knew what kind of person I was before I came to camp. So they learned relatively quickly.

I practiced as a quarterback for the rest of that week. Soon James, Jack and Tom came back, so I was relegated to strictly competing as a receiver, though I was still considered the emergency quarterback.

So I had 10 days to make the team as a wide receiver, a position I had never played or even given much thought. I realized the odds were very much against me. I had fulfilled my assigned role of filling in as quarterback while the other quarterbacks got healthy, and now, I had to learn a completely new position against the top percentage of receivers in the nation, men who had likely played receiver since midget ball.

"Oh, well, I have 10 days," I said to myself, "so I'll just do the best I can."

Though I had never run any patterns or anything, I did have good hands from playing basketball. I was a good athlete and a very, very quick study. I'd soak in all I could. Bill Miller, the former Oakland receiver, was the Bills receivers coach. He had great credentials. This quiet, subtle man took me under his wing. He maintained an even keel whether things went great or bad.

Coach Miller set out to show me the different ways to run patterns, running me through different drills. I sensed he was surprised that I could catch so well and that I had good footwork. In the first day of difficult catching drills, I really hung in there.

After that first day of intense receiving drills, Coach Miller pulled me over to the side.

"You did a great job today, Marlin," he said. "Actually, I'm kind of surprised. It's going to be tough for you to find a spot on this team in 10 days. But since you came in and did a good job of filling in and worked hard to learn receiver, we're not going to cut you right away."

He didn't know that when I signed my contract with Buffalo, I had insisted on another clause: Buffalo couldn't cut me until the final cut. That way, I'd have the best possible chance of making the team, and it also guaranteed that Buffalo wasn't just using me to be a quarterback for a week, and that I'd have a real opportunity to make the team as a receiver. That gave me my best shot, and the most available amount of time possible, to make the team. I knew if I had only a couple of days, I'd have to do everything right the first time—all the time—or I'd be gone. I'd have been pressing, and unsure of myself, which would have been a horrible atmosphere to perform in during such an important time in my career. So that contract stipulation was good to include.

Day by day, I improved. That constant improvement motivated me every day. I always went the extra mile, and I had to if I was going to make the team. I picked up some game film of the great receivers of that time, Paul Warfield and Lance Alworth—the best in pro ball. I'd study that film until bedcheck. I wanted to do all I could mentally and physically to learn the position, and, in turn, make the team. Both Warfield and Alworth liked to leap, and I realized that I had good leaping ability, and good timing. So while developing my own style to suit my strengths, I tried to emulate those guys. I also watched how they made their cuts, their moves, where they kept their hands, and how they caught the ball.

In the mornings, I'd always be eager for practice. And day by day I was getting better. I would have a shot in two exhibition games. The first one was against Cleveland.

But I didn't get in the game.

There were several other guys ahead of me in training camp, and I was the last one in, so it figured that they would get their shot.

Though I was running out of time and felt like I needed every possibility opportunity to make an impression, since the other guys had played in the other preseason games.

That meant it would all come down to one game, the final exhibition game, which would be followed a couple of days later by the final cut. Suddenly, I had just four days to make the team. I stepped up my regimen and prepared mentally for an even steeper learning curve. I was way, way down on the depth chart—out of view for all intense purposes. I had to make the most of every ball thrown to me. I had to catch it, whether it was a good throw or not. I leaped, I ran, I cut—I did whatever I could on every practice play and drill. Still, the guys in front of me had a lot more experience.

"So what," I would say to myself. "Don't give up without a fight. This could be it if you do."

I wouldn't think past that final sentence. I didn't want to ponder if I'd teach or whatever, because that wasn't an option. I'd go 100 percent with my entire focus on the final exhibition game.

We traveled to San Diego for that game. Jack Kemp was my roommate. The Bills always tried to put receivers with quarterbacks. I didn't know it at the time, but Jack had requested me as his roommate. He wasn't much taller than me, so he knew the real reason I wasn't given a chance at quarterback. And I don't believe Bob Griese was any taller either, come to think of it. At least we were within an inch of each other in terms of height.

The time with Jack was great.

"This is my last year in football," Kemp told me in the hotel. "After that, I'm planning to go into politics."

That didn't surprise me because Kemp was a great man, a fierce competitor and—as anyone who played with him would tell you— a phenomenal leader and organizer. On top of that, he was a sincerely nice person.

Talking to him, I started to pick up an underlying tone. He never came flat out and said it, but I realized that everything was going to work out just fine for me.

"I have to say that the improvement you've shown is amazing, Marlin," Jack said. "Just throwing the ball to you, I've noticed it. I appreciate your will. I respect the way you've persevered. No matter what happens, I admire the way you've stuck with it and fought back against the way you were treated after how well you performed last season. I know the chances of you making the team are slim, but you should be proud of yourself."

I saw this man as a great leader and felt fortunate to have him in my corner. O.J. Simpson was also in my corner. He noted my improvement and said I really stepped it up. I suppose they all thought they had to say good-bye to me and wish me well because it appeared my days were numbered—I just can't say for sure their reasons.

The next day, we took on the Chargers. I was on the bench through the entire first half. And again in the third quarter. The lights weren't completely out, but there wasn't a flicker either. My future with the Bills was dark.

Finally, as the fourth quarter wore on, Coach Rauch yelled, "Briscoe, get in there!"

My heart pounded through my chest. *Finally, an opportunity! My first chance to play receiver in my life, and I have to do this to make the team.*

Jack Kemp was in at quarterback. The first play he threw it to me, and I caught it. The next play, he threw it to me again. He kept throwing it to me, and I kept catching it. I'd do whatever it took, and some of the catches were of the highlight film quality as I jumped and dived. I was playing on adrenaline. Over the span of just a couple of minutes I caught four passes—every ball that was thrown at me, I hauled in. I led the team in receiving that game, in less than half a quarter of action.

My teammates were going wild. I got smacked so hard on the back, shoulders and helmet that I almost fell down a few times. I realized at that point that most of the team was actively, firmly, 100 percent behind me, and hoped I'd make the team. Everyone knew how hard I had worked and what I had gone through both in Denver, and then trying to learn a new position in just two weeks. Everyone congratulated me, even the receivers against whom I was competing.

And Jack Kemp was going nuts. He saw all this from afar and winked at me with that big smile of his. Though San Diego beat us—the Chargers were a very good team—it was preseason, and we had shown signs of improvement.

I knew that Jack had orchestrated that series of events—which he had intentionally thrown to me on every play he could. He wanted me to make the team so badly. He had a lot of confidence in me even though I hadn't played the position before. That, to me, was the ultimate compliment.

Though I had given the team a shot in the arm, my football career was still on life support. The jury was still out though with the final cut coming up immediately. The Bills had to decide to keep me or keep some of the experienced players, guys who had played the position for a long time and had reputations as solid, if perhaps unspectacular, performers.

Quite honestly, even though I was in a whirlwind, I figured I would be cut. I knew that one good preseason performance didn't give you a green light to continue your career. I also knew that if I didn't make the team, my career as a professional football player was over. I couldn't and wouldn't go back to Canada, and since I hadn't heard from other NFL teams, that wasn't an option, either.

In years to come, I would find out that some very, very special players on that team had lobbied to the coaches for me.

Lo and behold, I made the final roster. No, it wasn't at quarterback. But I don't know that I had a prouder moment athletically in my life, learning the new position and fitting in—pretty good for the guy who had possibly been labeled a bad apple coming out of Denver.

I called my mother, and Rick Davis, who had suggested months earlier in his insurance office that I play receiver. There I was, a NFL receiver, just months later.

At least one or two more experienced receivers were let go in favor of keeping me. That was too bad because even though you compete against each other to make the team, you build a bond and there's respect there.

Since I had made the cut, it was time to get ready for the first game of the season. James Harris was prepared to become the first black quarterback to start the season. James—whose nickname is "Shack" something I call him to this day—asked that I would be his roommate. We had a common bond, and I could help him as far as what he'd have to endure what the questions would be.

We had good conversations about it, just awesome, deep conversations that we enjoyed—and treasured, really. Here I had paved the way for James and those to follow, and now, less than a year after paving that way, I was literally showing the way to my teammate. As it would turn out, almost everything that I told James would happen that year did—some good, some bad.

We opened the season with the Jets. We came out of the gates slow and were beaten very soundly. James, being a rookie, had to have a learning curve. He had come from Grambling where the legendary Eddie Robinson was coaching. That was an all-black school, whereas I had been at a predominantly white school and league, so I didn't have the kind of culture shock that Shack would experience for the first time.

Shack is a very smart man. His intelligence is astounding to those who know him. But he was quiet, almost to the point of being shy, around those he didn't know well. I think a lot of that came from the fact that he had grown up in Louisiana during a very turbulent time for that state, and the South. James was wary of his new surroundings in the NFL team, and of having to lead a predominantly white group of athletes for the first time. And Buffalo's players were being led for the first time by a black man, so there would be a period of transition to endure on all fronts.

After the game James was very frustrated. We talked late into the night as I related to him the tough times that I had endured during my time in Denver. I pointed out that I had come back to have a stellar rookie year. He was 6-foot-4, 220 pounds, so he could certainly turn his season around.

There were a lot of rumblings in Buffalo, though. James received some death threats, something I never had to deal with. He was understandably devastated by those threats.

James was a very sensitive, kind-hearted man. He was a great quarterback in the making, a real diamond in the rough. Physically, he was both strong and imposing. With his size, no NFL personnel guy could say that James wasn't big enough—as they did with me to demean my ability.

However, the critics—or hypocrites, if you will—used a similarly inane reason, claiming James threw too hard. I couldn't believe it when I heard that. Haven Moses and I—and all of the other receivers—never had any problem catching his passes. Sure, he had a strong arm, but to even imply that he threw the ball too hard was absurd. In years to come, that would be shown to be a ridiculous, baseless criticism, because Hall of Fame bound John Elway threw bullets, and he wasn't benched because of it.

I started to sense that the criticism would continue to mount, and that Buffalo would soon find more reasons to look for another quarterback. The first excuse that he was a hard thrower was followed by equally ludicrous comments that he wasn't intelligent enough for the position. I suppose that kind of chatter was generated because he wasn't a loudmouth. Those who got to know him knew that he was one of the funniest, most articulate people you'd ever meet, and a great storyteller.

Sometimes, people who don't talk a lot have their intelligence questioned—when in reality it should be those who are doing the questioning that are lined up for IQ tests.

James was growing more discouraged. He couldn't understand—and correctly didn't agree—with those criticisms. He very much understood that he needed to continue to improve, as would any rookie.

Another who struggled at the beginning of the year was O.J. Simpson. He came out the most heralded college running back ever. He didn't endear himself to Buffalo's fans when he said he wanted to play in San Francisco where he grew up, or with the then Los Angeles Rams, which was a more glamorous setting. The fans would get irate. Of course, anyone who knows O.J. knew he just said things that he didn't mean. There was a problem with his philosophy and John Rauch's philosophy. They had a great passing game with the Raiders, and used the running game only to complement the passing game, and that carried over to Buffalo.

Coach Rauch wanted to use O.J. as a receiver out of the backfield. But we didn't have the personnel that the Raiders did for the kind of offense Rauch wanted. O.J. and Coach Rauch were oil and vinegar from the get-go. It was clear that unless we made the playoffs or showed a lot of improvement, one of them would have to go eventually. O.J. was frustrated. It wasn't that O.J. or Rauch were either blatantly wrong. It was just two very different agendas and attitudes. Regardless, it didn't endear O.J. to Coach Rauch.

Back in those days, our offensive line wasn't as big or talented as the Raiders' line had been, so there wouldn't have been a lot of big holes for O.J. to run through even if we had shifted to a run-oriented offense.

Still, O.J. wore his heart on his sleeve—his just lost his shirt too often! However, he never did get in a shouting match with Coach or anything like that. O.J. and I lived in the same apartment building and got to know each other. He'd become agitated telling us how he hated the offense and Coach Rauch.

In that first game, I didn't play but a couple of plays, and had no balls thrown to me. O.J. was bottled up, and the offense just wasn't successful. Bubba Thorton, a white guy who could flat out run, started ahead of me at receiver. He had been a track star at Texas Christian and had even tried out at the Olympic Trials. But Bubba wasn't an accomplished receiver. Though he was much faster than I was, he had only a little bit more experience as a receiver than I did, which was to say, not that much. The guy was a team player through and through, though, and taught me how to run faster.

But the coaches quickly saw that he wasn't productive, and he wouldn't be the kind of complement to free up Haven. Haven would get double-teamed and the other team would practically let Bubba go, knowing he didn't have good hands and didn't run solid routes. So the coaches changed for the second game, saying that Bubba would play the first half, and I would play the second half.

Seeing limited action in the second half in both our second and third games, I had already amassed eight catches. It shifted even more, with Bubba starting and playing the first quarter, with me playing the final three. I improved week to week. I was ahead of Bubba in both receptions and productions, and Haven was getting free more often, a big goal of the coaches because of Haven's considerable talent.

I was also endeared to my teammates more because I was a very good blocker. O.J. knew that if he could break free at the line of scrimmage that he'd have at least one fewer guy to worry about in the secondary because I would do my job.

After about the sixth week, I was approached by three great guys: Jack Kemp, James Harris, and Paul Maguire, who was the punter (and a former linebacker) on our team, but commanded a lot of respect and was one of our leaders because of his work ethic and how he carried himself.

One of them asked, "Why do you think you aren't starting when you're doing better than the guy ahead of you?"

I remembered—and was aware—that one of the clauses in my contract said that if I started half the games in the 14-game season, I would get a $1,500 salary bonus, raising my pay from $16,000 to $17,500 for the season.

They looked at me and almost chuckled. My contract, for a guy who had set a club record the year before and been named runner-up rookie of the year, wasn't exactly a vault of gold. But beggars can't be choosers. And after all, I was learning a new position.

When I told them about the clause, they were appalled that I wasn't starting possibly just because of the bonus. That such a thing was possible hadn't crossed my mind until those guys brought it to my attention—after all, why not start someone who gives your team a better chance of winning? Those three guys were among a group that went to Coach Rauch and essentially said that they would stage some sort of protesting if I didn't get to start.

After lobbying on my behalf, I got the start. The Raiders had a star defensive back that I would be facing, Kent McCloughan, an all-pro who had played at the University of Nebraska. He had been a state high school sprint champion and a great player. I was so pumped to be starting, both because of what my teammates had done, and because I was facing McCloughan, one of the league's toughest bump and run cornerbacks.

I had the biggest game of my career to that point. I had, I believe, 140 yards in receptions, including a 66-yarder for one of my two touchdown catches. After the game McCloughan and I were able to talk, visiting briefly about our days in Nebraska.

I ended up starting the rest of the year for the Bills, thus earning the bonus money.

The money ended up being far from the highlight because on the field I led the AFC in catches. The players and fans and media in Buffalo voted me as the team's Most Valuable Offensive player, over the likes of O.J. Simpson and Haven Moses. O.J. didn't get anywhere close to 1,000 yards that year, and had very few touchdowns. Those weren't the numbers he had been hoping for.

Bills teammate Ben Gregory, from the University of Nebraska, O.J. and I were close that year. We road-tripped to Toronto occasionally to get away from everything. O.J.'s wife and young child were back in California. One day, O.J. talked about quitting. He had planned it out in his mind, just going back to California and finding something good to do back there, to be with his family. Granted, O.J. talked sometimes just to hear his own voice. But he seemed serious that day, quite depressed. I told him, "Look at what happened to me. Look how I ended up in Buffalo. I've resurrected my career at a different position. Life is not a continuum." O.J. took that to heart and said he'd wait the season out. Like I said, I'm not sure how close he was to packing up his bags and heading across the country. But I knew him fairly well by that time, and since there was no crowd around—meaning his comments were more thought out than off the cuff—I took him as being totally serious. So I believe I helped him keep his career on track at that critical fork in the road.

That season, we played our final game in Los Angeles. O.J. lived in L.A., of course. James Harris, Bills defensive back Booker Edgerson and I decided to go to Las Vegas. O.J. was an avid dice thrower. We used to do that and play cards in our apartments during the cold Buffalo winter. O.J. was the luckiest guy I knew. He'd always draw the exact card he needed, or get the precise number he need to win at dice. I called him "Midas." On a trip to Vegas the previous year, O.J. had apparently won a lot of money for a lot of people, including a man who owned a textile factory. O.J. introduced us around, and we had a good time.

But "Midas" didn't have his touch that day. He lost all the money he had brought (this was long before the day of the ATM machine), and even another $300 that I loaned him.

He said he'd pay me back right away when he got back to Los Angeles. But I had to get straight to Omaha because I had a job with parks and rec. lined up for the summer. He called me when I got home, wanting to know where to send the money.

"Listen, I'm having a sports clinic for kids in Omaha," I told him. "Don't send the money. You can pay me back by coming out for my clinic."

The sports clinic was, ironically, in the Bryan Center, where I had snapped my neck entering my senior year at Omaha University.

O.J. said "no problem," and came out. He ate my mother's cooking and met a lot of folks in Omaha, and everyone just loved him. You have to remember—and those who aren't yet in their mid-30s probably can't—that back in the 1970s, O.J. was the most recognized athlete in the country for a time, and a popular pitchman for endorsement deals. The city really embraced O.J. during his three-day visit.

Though I had put up some good numbers during my first year with the Bills, I knew I had a lot of room to improve. I hadn't even put a full year of experience as a receiver under my belt—much less at the professional level—so it was time to close the gap on my performance, and potential, at receiver.

Since I wasn't going to be a "stop-gap" quarterback in training camp entering my second year, I was able to focus on only wide receiver. I dedicated myself to improving my speed. I was always quick, but never had blazing speed. I never ran track that much whereas most wide receivers, especially in college and the pros, had been track standouts.

So learning how to run properly—there's a very scientific technique to it—and becoming properly conditioned (each position in football has particular conditioning needs) were important. I spent hours and days—weeks even—running hills in North Omaha. I'd get anyone I could to throw passes to me. Again, guys from my college and the semi-pro Omaha Mustangs were of invaluable assistance for that.

To improve my speed and running, George Anderson, a world-class sprinter who played for the Mustangs, helped me, and really improved my speed.

Finally, I entered a training camp for the first time in my pro career in the best physical shape for the position I was to play that season. Knowing I was going to be a receiver also helped my mental approach. And I knew I had earned a space on the team, though I thrived on the fact that I'd still have to compete to earn my spot. I was in the best shape I'd been in my life, mentally and physically.

Concern did surround my good friend James Harris. It was clear when the Bills drafted Dennis Shaw with their first pick out of San Diego State. That made it obvious that James wasn't the Bills' quarterback of either the present or future. That reminded me so much of how I felt after my first year with the Broncos. James wasn't slighted like I was with Denver in the regard that no "secret" meetings were held without inviting him. Still, it smelled of the entire Pete Liske scenario. I had told James when we roomed together for the 1969 season that a situation exactly like this could develop—I wished I would have been wrong on that one.

James did go through the meetings and was well prepared. There was a lot of fanfare about Dennis Shaw, as there should have been because he was a good quarterback. He didn't throw the ball with a lot of zip—he sort of floated it, but the guy was a winner.

At training camp, Dennis Shaw, like Jack Kemp, showed a lot of confidence in me. Dennis and I just meshed. He threw a lot of balls soft in the air, and I had to make circus catches. I had played a lot of basketball that summer, and going up for Shaw's passes was like going up for rebounds some of the time. I made a few leaping grabs in camp early, and Shaw quickly developed a lot of confidence in me. He threw good passes, but they were more touch passes than on a line. Either way worked for me—just get the ball my way, and I'd gladly go after it regardless of how it got there.

Right before the season, teams make their final cut. That was the one I had to sweat out the previous year before I made the Bills as a receiver.

James was sent packing that week. Since I had been so close to James, I left camp with him that final day to show my support for him. That could have been a big mistake on my part, but I had to support James. I didn't get in any trouble, but I really, really could have.

I talked to James. Honestly, I had seen the writing on the wall. As I said, the same sort of thing had happened to me. James didn't really believe me when I told him that just such a scenario could unfold—and I certainly didn't say, "I told you so." James actually thanked me for sharing my experiences and thoughts. James had thought that my size was the reason I was shoved out of Denver's quarterback picture. Clearly, that wasn't what I believed; I thought it had to do with race.

James headed back home. We started the season with Dennis Shaw as the quarterback. James was clearly better than the backup quarterbacks we kept were. But the Bills didn't want to risk the controversy and distractions that might have resulted from keeping James as a backup to the rookie quarterback. If Shaw had faltered and James was to come in and perform well, it would have showed Buffalo had made a mistake.

In pro football—and in life—you have people leave, or get fired, and you have to focus on doing your job. I had a good situation developing in Buffalo. The 1970 season would be a banner year for me. I led the entire AFL in receiving and made all-pro—the only member of the Bills to make it that year. O.J. Simpson didn't make it that year, and neither did Haven Moses, our top receiver when I was brought to the team.

O.J. Simpson had a lot of clout on those teams, especially after his rookie season. We were watching films during the 1970 season. O.J. could get a guy cut just by making some comment in the film study. This happened a couple of times, where O.J. had pointed out that so-and-so had missed a block or wasn't making a play, and that guy had been gone within a few hours. It freaked some people out as we took notice that O.J. had this kind of power, to get guys cut on the spot.

There was a big tight end named Willie Great from North Carolina A&T. He was a backup who played mostly on special teams. Our starting tight end was Billy Masters, so Great came in only on certain downs because he could run the deep patterns very well for a tight end. But there was no question that his value was on special teams.

We were watching films one week, and there was a play where Willie hadn't quite gotten his block completed. The coaches hadn't come in yet, and were due any second.

"You see that?" O.J. said, "Our man Willie Great missed that one!"

All of the sudden, a huge shadow moved toward the door. On went the lights.

"Don't you be messing with my paycheck, O.J. Simpson," Great bellowed, shaking up all of us, most notably O.J. "You ain't going after my money, you understand? You stay away from my paycheck!"

With this large, irate man shaking his finger and threatening to shake his world, O.J. just quietly nodded. As I recall, the coaches were there maybe 10 minutes later, and we had a nice, quiet film study. And Great stayed on the team. Many of us laughed at that story later in the day. That was certainly an interesting way to get job security. But it worked.

My best games during that season were against the Miami Dolphins, who were building a team that would in years to come become the best, arguably among the top in NFL history. I had two touchdowns and broke 100 yards in receiving in each of the two games that season against our AFC East rivals. Even though the Dolphins had a great defense, they just couldn't contain me.

I was excited, and honored, to go to Los Angeles to play in the Pro Bowl. The format was the AFL against the NFL. The quarterback for our team was Darryl Lamonica from the Oakland Raiders. Oakland's Raymond Chester was our tight end and Raider Warren Wells was the left side starting wide receiver. I was the starting wide receiver on the right side, with Oakland's Fred Biletnikoff. I was flattered to beat out Biletnikoff for the starting spot, as he would end up in the Hall of Fame.

Dennis Shaw was selected the Rookie of the Year. I heard from a lot of people that I helped make that happen, as Shaw's numbers were boosted by my numbers—just as he boosted my numbers.

"You made Dennis the rookie of the year," O.J. Simpson told me.

I wasn't that self-absorbed. Sure, I did make some difficult, highlight reel type catches, but I was also rewarded.

So 1969 and 1970 were a period of great accomplishment for me, as a player who had never logged a down at receiver before taking up the position two years earlier. Going to the Pro Bowl was another memorable experience.

11

Telling Al Davis "No"

At the Pro Bowl practice, I worked hard. After the first practice, Al Davis, the owner of the Raiders, came up to me.

"You had a hell of year, kid," Mr. Davis told me. "You almost beat me as a quarterback a couple years ago, and then in two years you make it to the Pro Bowl as a receiver. I've never seen anything like that."

"Thank you, Mr. Davis," I said, affording proper respect to the icon he had already become in the sport.

He stopped when we were out of earshot of anyone else.

"I want you to do me a favor," Davis said.

"What's that, Mr. Davis?" I asked.

"I have Warren on one side, Raymond at tight end, Lamonica on the other," he said, " so if you'd let Biletnikoff start ahead of you, the whole lineup of quarterbacks and receivers would be Raiders. What do you say?"

I didn't even think about it.

"No, Mr. Davis," I said. "I can't do that. I earned the spot."

No one ever said "no" to Al Davis. I had heard a lot of stories about how he'd carry grudges for years and years. Don't get me wrong, because I respected his impressive list of accomplishments. But, I had worked hard and overcome a lot of adversity to get to that position.

"I don't know if I'll ever make it again, Mr. Davis," I told him.

"I'm going to savor this moment. I'm going to start, because I earned it."

Quite frankly, he didn't appreciate me turning him down. I think years later, it would affect me as my career wound down prematurely.

The practice was manipulated to get Biletnikoff more repetitions than me.

I also met some really great people whose path I would cross in the years to come. Bob Griese was the Pro Bowl backup quarterback for our team, and his Miami teammate, Paul Warfield, was a backup receiver. Since Biletnikoff ended up getting so many reps in practice, I ended up on the other side quite a bit, where Warfield was, and where Griese was logging most of his practice at the Pro Bowl. I really got to know those guys a bit.

I ended up leading the AFL in receptions for the Pro Bowl, and really enjoyed playing with both Warfield and Griese. They were two great people, and as far as I was concerned, their ability as players was exceeded by the quality of character they displayed. Coach Don Shula saw how effectively I worked with his players, Warfield and Griese.

My relationship with the Bills, though, didn't improve. I thought I would be rewarded with a new contract. In fact, to collect my $1,500 bonus from the year before, I ended up having to drive to Detroit on my way back to Omaha to collect the money. I couldn't believe how hard they made it for me to collect that money, refusing to pay me in a timely manner. So Bills' owner Ralph Wilson—for all the great things he did in Buffalo, and for the sport—was never one of my personal favorites.

Since I had made all-pro, worked hard and learned a new position, I thought the new contract would be upcoming. I asked for a contract of $25,000 for the 1972 season, up from the $16,000 I had made the previous year. I felt like I was already thousands of dollars behind after getting pushed out of Denver, and then working for a relatively meager salary my first two years in Buffalo. The Bills countered with an offer of $18,500. In short, I wasn't getting anywhere near market value.

In 1971, I went through camp hoping the contract would get resolved. Nothing happened. I didn't complain or anything, but I wanted a fair market contract. Ralph Wilson and his negotiators still wouldn't give me a fair contract. They had paid Dennis Shaw all of this money—and he deserved it—but I thought I should be recognized contractually as well.

We were getting ready to open the season at War Memorial Stadium. I decided that I'd rather not play if I didn't have my contract squabble worked out.

Training camp had, of course, ended, and I was staying at a hotel about a half-mile from the stadium because I didn't have an apartment. If I were going to be offered a contract worth only $2,500 more than the previous year, I would sit out. I always stuck up for myself. However, in those days, when you stood up for yourself, you were labeled a malcontent, especially if you were right, and black.

I guess the coaches didn't believe I'd stick by my guns. O.J. Simpson and Paul Maguire knew where I was, and what was going on. They supported me and knew it was unfair.

Two hours before kickoff, I heard a knock on my door. Maguire and O.J., who had more experience and clout with the Bills, were looking for me.

"We need you to play out your contract," Maguire said. "Financially, it won't be rewarding here in Buffalo. No matter what you sign, you'll be stuck with a substandard contract on a bad team. Just play out this year, and you'll be a free agent after the season ends. Then, you can go where you want to go."

The Bills had two promising young receivers in Bobby Chandler and J.D. Hill. The Bills thought they could get along without me. Bobby was my closest competitor. He challenged me every day for my job, and it was fierce competition, which I thrived on. The competition made us both better. Bobby and I became very close friends. Haven was being challenged on the other side by J.D.

I thought about what Maguire said. He was a smart, strong man, and very sensible. I said, "Well, my way isn't the right way, at least not now, even though I'm right." The Bills already had someone ready to take my place, which is how it works in pro sports.

So I went to the stadium, got dressed, went out and played. It was my option year, which meant the team held the option. I decided I'd just do the best that I could that season, keep abreast of the market value and not let my contract differences with Ralph Wilson and the Buffalo Bills keep me from proving I was a two-year fluke.

Shaw didn't have the type of season he had the year before. We didn't throw the ball as much as we had the year before. O.J. still didn't reach the 1,000-yard mark, a standard—whether fair or unfair—by which great backs are measured. Coach Rauch had resigned after the 1970 season, and Harvey Johnson had taken over. Harvey didn't have a lot of coaching experience, because he had been a front office guy.

Yet we had more talent than the year before. Still, we went just 1-13 in 1971. It was chaos on the team, from management on down. I couldn't believe that with all the talent we had that we won just one game that year.

In 1971 while playing out my option year in Buffalo, I was approached by a group of about 30 players who wanted to challenge the legality of a rule that we thought was unfair, and applied directly to me. We had no real free agency in those days. If your contract was up, you either took the contract the team offered you, or you sat out. Certainly, you could ask for a raise. But if you didn't get it, you had no option of looking somewhere else. The rule was that if Team A had a veteran free agent, and Team B signed the player, then Team A was entitled to "fair and equitable" compensation from Team B. That kept the veteran without a contract stuck with his old team, and no bargaining power for a raise, or to find a better situation by moving teams. This rule, in itself, prohibited free agency. NFL Commissioner Pete Rozelle—arguably the strongest, most powerful league director in the history of sports—or at least his office, decided what compensation your previous team would get from the team with whom you signed.

Many will remember Baltimore Colts standout tight end John Mackey because he basically defined the position of tight end for the modern era of professional football. But he was also the signature person on the Rozelle Rule lawsuit. Mackey was the first president of the NFL Players Association after the AFL and NFL merged in 1968.

Rozelle, or his office, making the judgment about compensation for teams was ridiculously one-sided toward the owners. It was a very arbitrary decision. And since Rozelle was employed by the team owners to run their league, you can easily see whose interest Rozelle had at heart—it certainly wasn't the player. The Rozelle Rule discouraged other teams from signing players, which in turn forced players to stay with their teams and accept whatever contract they were offered. It also discouraged other teams from signing players away from their original teams because they could lose anything that Rozelle chose to take away from them. In later years, such labor practices would burn baseball.

But at the time, I signed on. Slowly but very surely—and for obvious reasons of coercion—players dropped from the lawsuit like flies. Players who weren't front-line starters were dropped from their teams like hot potatoes, though some who acquiesced and dropped their role in the suit found homes with teams—though some didn't.

But the owners would remember that I was a part of that suit. Perhaps not that day, but definitely in the years to come.

So back in Buffalo, after playing my final year of the contract, things were about to change. That forgetful season took its toll. When a team wins just one game throughout the course of the season—especially with the talent we had—frustrations build, and boil over. The Bills were a ragtag organization at that point. That was the worst experience of my career as far as a season, from start to finish. I did have several good games, doing what I could to play through all the distractions and discord. I wasn't an all-pro, but I did my job well.

I wasn't sure, but I suspected, that I was on my way out of Buffalo. The Bills hired a new coach.

Lou Saban, my old nemesis.

"How can this happen?" I thought to myself.

I had finally gotten past all of the negativity and vile actions that had pushed me out of Denver—rebuilt my career on the field and been a pillar in the community—and into the picture comes Lou Saban.

Think I was on my way out? Yes, you are right.

Since the club basically owned me, they could trade me if I turned down their contract offer. I joke that Saban probably traded me on his plane ride to Buffalo.

Paul Maguire was the ultimate jokester, the funniest football player I ever met. He had a quip about everything. The things he said might be offensive to other people, but to those of us who knew him, he was amazingly humorous. He parlayed that personality to a great career as a broadcaster. He rode O.J. pretty hard—but it was in good nature, because they hung out together, and we all played cards and those kinds of things. We'd take the white guys to the ghetto to eat soul food—War Memorial Stadium was in the ghetto, so we'd go eat after we were done at the stadium.

In Buffalo, we were more of a family unit off the field. As I would learn later, that was not critical to having a successful team, though I didn't yet grasp that while in Buffalo.

Another member of that Bills team was Robert James, a cornerback, who had gone to school in Tennessee, and was very religious. Robert once quit the team because someone was cursing in the locker room. Robert and I went against each other hard in practice. So much so that by the time we got through with each other in practice, the games were easy.

We had receiver J.D. Hill, who actually brought his own tailor from Arizona State. J.D. was one of the wildest guys I ever met. Everyone on the team, James Harris, O.J.—even the white guys—went from our traditional suits to "pimp" clothes, polyester suits with the big, wide-brimmed hats. It was funny to see.

I can't overstate what great guys Flores and Kemp were. Tom Flores was an extremely intelligent quarterback and we've played some golf together since. But by the time I got to Buffalo, he had a big scar on his shoulder from surgery, so his arm wasn't as strong as it had once been. But I was amazed at how well he knew the game.

As I've stated about Kemp, he was one of the nicest people I ever met. When he ran for the Senate in Buffalo, Spiro Agnew came to speak, as both were Republicans. Spiro was the opposite of what I stood for, in terms of politics. Jack asked O.J. and I to be at that event. The only reason O.J. and I went was because of Jack, and the fondness and respect we had for Jack. He appreciated us going, because he knew how we felt about Spiro Agnew.

Since I was headed out of Buffalo, I decided to get an agent for the first time in my career. I had done fine for myself to that point, but the factors out of my control—and since the money was escalating—made it more prudent to get someone to do that for me, which took a lot of stress off of my mind.

That summer, I went to Los Angeles and worked out, waiting to see where Saban would send me. I had a great time representing the NFL on a tour of Vietnam as part of an offshoot of the Bob Hope Troupe. I didn't go to Vietnam as a soldier. I had flunked my physical. I never believed in that war, but I never blamed the troops who had to go. They were doing what they had to for their country, and I respected that. I thought going over to boost moral was an honor for me.

We went to Vietnam for 10 days. It was an experience like no other. War was still going on, and we visited several bases. We went up in helicopters and were allowed to fire M-16s. At several of the bases closer to the front, we could hear shooting at times. There was a constant threat of danger even though we were there on a goodwill mission. I was so proud of our American soldiers for the courage they showed. Courage isn't going over the middle to catch as a pass as a defender lines you up to knock you senseless. Courage is going to a foreign land to give your life for your country.

The harsh reality never escaped me during the trip that it could very easily have been me there. When we were at Da Nang, the situation was high alert. Several military officials came in and stopped us from eating to check our food. It turned out that the enemy had gotten in and poisoned the ice for the drinks. That check saved a lot of lives, including my own.

I left Vietnam and took a job while I worked out in Los Angeles. I spent a lot of time with O.J. Simpson and fellow Bills teammate Al "A.C." Cowlings, since I knew I wouldn't be playing with them ever again.

My agent called one day.

"How would you like to play with the Dolphins?" he asked.

The Dolphins were known to be a great organization that treated their players well. On top of that, they were proven winners and the thought of contending for a championship was very appealing.

It was well known during the 1972 Super Bowl (actually from the 1971 season, but the Super Bowl was played in January 16, 1972) that the Dallas Cowboys had double-covered Miami star receiver Paul Warfield, and that the other receiver, Howard Twilley, hadn't produced enough as offense-less Miami was pounded, 24-3. The Dolphins thought they needed a receiver on the other side to take the pressure off Paul. And they thought I was that receiver.

"You've got to be kidding," I told my agent.

"No," he said, "Coach Shula called."

The Dolphins offered me far more money I had asked for in Buffalo.

So I became a Miami Dolphin. To avoid having to let the Rozelle Rule take its course, Shula traded a first-round draft pick to get me. That way, the deal was done. Had Shula just signed me, Rozelle could have determined whatever he wanted for Buffalo to receive in return. Since I had been an all-pro receiver, he could have made Miami give Buffalo his all-pro receiver, Paul Warfield, and then had no recourse to undo it. Shula's move was a preemptive strike, and it worked in circumventing the Rozelle Rule.

So Lou Saban, unwittingly, helped me make history in two areas. First of all, I became the first black quarterback to start and play regularly in pro football. Secondly, because of his decision not to invite me to quarterback camp and not let me compete for the position, I was traded to Buffalo and eventually to Miami, where I would be a part of the only undefeated team in NFL history. All of that being said—and I am still pained by the memories of how I was treated to this day—I never came out and took Saban to task publicly. I could have, and I think I would have been on solid ground to do so. My belief always was to do my talking on the field in the manner of letting my play speak for itself.

I loved it in Miami, from the first day. And in the 1972 season, we—the Dolphins—were going to make history.

The season started with a win over Kansas City. Quarterback Bob Griese picked up right where he left off the previous season. I caught Miami's first touchdown pass of the year in the game against the Chiefs. I also pushed Twilley, who improved greatly from last season. I've always said I enjoy the challenge of competing for a spot. And clearly, one of the reasons Coach Shula brought me was to both complement Warfield, and help Howard Twilley get even better.

As I look back, we had more talent in Buffalo, but we didn't have that team-first attitude. And we didn't have that organization and professionalism that Coach Shula brought. His attention to detail and conditioning was the best I had seen. I had heard before coming to Miami about how tough Shula's training camps were—they were that, and more. But it was worth it. Paul Warfield's influence on me was profound. This was a guy who—though he didn't know it—had taught me how to play receiver while I watched film of him during my transition to receiver that first camp in Buffalo. Watching him in practice was awesome, and I learned so much working with him every day. We became best friends.

We beat Buffalo badly that season. I made sure that after the game, I made eye contact with Saban. I went up as close as I could get and I smiled at him. The look of derision he cast at me said it all. Obviously, he wasn't happy that we beat them. I just wasn't about to go away. I survived the four-day wait and his release, and I made all-pro in Buffalo. And now, I was part of the greatest football team in the league, the Miami Dolphins, and we had just crushed the Bills.

In the fourth game of the year, I pulled a hamstring, something I trace all the way back to that first summer of getting ready for pro ball when I overtrained, and then pulled a hamstring in Broncos' camp. This time, Howard Twilley came in and played well. Of course, we were still undefeated, mowing teams down each week.

No one really noticed that we were undefeated until the tenth week of the season when we went to New York. The New York media really seized on the undefeated angle, and it became national news. Within our team, we realized something very special might be happening.

What a group of talent on the Dolphins: just to list a few (and all are deserving), we had Griese, Warfield, Jim Kiick, Mercury Morris and Larry Csonka on offense, and our famed "No-name" defense had a group of special players, all overachievers in their own right.

When my hamstring mended, Coach Shula came to me. I know the rule is that players can't lose a starting spot due to an injury. But team chemistry is also important. On that Miami team, we had no egos, despite all that talent. We all suppressed our individual agendas for the betterment of the team. Warfield and Griese were perfect examples. The running backs would have been featured stars on any other team, but they gladly molded themselves into a merciless three-headed monster that left opposing defenses scratching their heads. A lot of stars gladly accepted second-team status in addition to help the team. All wanted to start, of course, but it was team first.

With that in mind, Coach Shula came to me.

"Howard is playing well, and you played well before he was hurt, but we don't want to upset the apple cart with the way things are going," Shula said.

"I certainly understand that, Coach," I said with a smile.

Howard would play the first half, and I would play the second half. I played effectively and put up some good numbers. We didn't have to pass a tremendous amount because of that immensely talented backfield, though Griese made the most of every toss. All of the receivers could block really well. It was a beautiful exhibition of team sport.

We rolled undefeated through the regular season at 14-0, and the eyes of the football world were focused clearly upon us. We faced Pittsburgh in the playoffs. I was completely healthy, but Howard Twilley got the start and most of the action because he had playoff experience. I wanted to do only what was best for the team. I was the only big off-season addition from the 1971 team that had made it to the Super Bowl (a 24-3 loss to Dallas). And Howard really stepped up, responded to the challenge and played well.

I didn't get in during the playoffs until Super Bowl VII, which was against the Washington Redskins on Jan. 14, 1973.

We had this special play we practiced involving Washington's Pat Fischer, the brother of one my favorite coaches ever, Ken Fischer, who coached me at Omaha University. I grew up just idolizing Pat. And Ken had helped me make the transition to receiver that summer before I joined Buffalo. Heading into the Super Bowl, Coach Shula's staff saw something they could take advantage of against Pat. Howard scored in the Super Bowl where he beat Pat to put us up 7-0.

But Howard pulled his hamstring, and I was thrust into action. The play that we worked on all week was to get me—or Howard—to isolate Pat, to get him to cover me and thus free up Warfield. Everything was set up perfectly.

However, at the line of scrimmage, I couldn't hear Griese calling out the count. I have to admit I was somewhat nervous. I knew I should have been watching the ball and forgot about trying to hear Griese and the snap count. I went just a hair offsides and hoped the official didn't see me. The play unfolded perfectly, and Griese hit an open Warfield for a touchdown.

A flag was thrown. Off-sides, Miami—me.

The play was called back. I was hurting inside, fearing I would cost my team the game. Coach Shula met me before I could get back to the sideline. He's a very intense person, and I can't repeat what he said. But I deserved it for making a silly, costly mistake in the biggest game of the year.

Nobody was more hurt than I was. To see the expression on my teammates' faces hurt me. I had let them down. Warfield came over to me.

"Come on, it's all right," he said. "We're going to get them."

Even with a bum leg, Twilley was put back into the game, and I was benched. A lot of people don't remember that play because of our kicker, Garo Yepremian's much replayed play, where he tried to throw the ball on a disastrous muffed field-goal attempt, and Washington's Mike Bass grabbed the ball and ran 49 yards for a touchdown. Instead of winning 17-0 (assuming Garo made that field goal), we won 14-7 as Bass' score was Washington's only points.

Still, we were 17-0 that season.

17-0!

But I remembered my play. To this day, it's hard for me to fathom that I made a mistake so big that it could have cost us a Super Bowl.

I took that mistake as personal motivation to come back and win my job back the next season. I knew what I had to do. I stayed in Los Angeles with friends. I wanted to soothe my wounds. I wasn't in a very good mood even though we won the Super Bowl. I was happy about winning the Super Bowl, but that one play haunted me.

I went back to Nebraska on my way back to Miami. I trained like the dickens, stairs, on the track, running all kinds of sprints at different distances. I knew we could win another Super Bowl, and I wanted to be a part of it if Coach Shula wanted me back.

Howard Twilley was, of course, the starter ahead of me going into camp. But he pulled a hamstring and I stepped in, with Howard out several weeks. We were playing well during the 1973 season as we tried to repeat as Super Bowl champions. When Howard came back, Shula was consistent.

"We're playing well, you're doing a very good job, and we're winning," Coach Shula said, telling me I would remain the starter, just as he had kept Twilley the starter the year before when I pulled a hamstring. Shula was among the fairest men in pro sports. And to give me a chance to redeem myself after possibly costing our team the Super Bowl the year before also said a lot about his character, and belief in the players he brought in for his team.

For the season, I led Miami in receiving. That meant so much, especially coming off the Super Bowl miscue.

And I had an outstanding game in Super Bowl VIII, a 24-7 win over the Minnesota Vikings. I tied for a team high with two catches, and didn't make any mistakes in terms of penalties as I had the previous year.

My friends and teammates were so glad I had shaken that 500-pound gorilla off my back.

Because of my labor representative experience, I was nominated by my Miami teammates to be the alternate behind Doug Swift for the upcoming 1974 negotiations with the owners for a collective bargaining agreement. The Dolphins, as Super Bowl champions, were the focus of a lot of coverage for the labor discussions. To try to gain leverage, we decided not to play an annual all-star game, in which the Super Bowl champions—which that year would have been us, the Dolphins—played a group of college all-stars, with the money going to charity. The game, which had been a much-publicized annual event, was never played again. The issue was turned into a black/white issue.

Even though many of us black players were on the picket line in 1974—after the 1973 season—most of our union reps were white. So the black players bore the brunt of criticism since pictures and TV footage included mostly black players. I believe the owners manipulated some of the media coverage—Rozelle had a complete hold over the media, as Howard Cosell often pointed out—to antagonize America against us.

The pension plan was the focus point of the labor discussions. That was the real issue, and still is today, because the NFL's pension plan was for a long time not up to snuff compared to other sports, and even other businesses.

The Dolphins didn't play ball that way. They just wanted to get better every year. In 1974, Miami drafted Nat Moore out of the University of Florida. He was going to be pressing me for the job. I was entering the final year of a three-year contract. Nat had been a heralded running back and a Miami native. So there was a lot of competition with him, Howard Twilley and me. So, I worked hard and won the starting job. Nat had injured his knee during training camp. So, once again, I was the starter.

I started the 1974 season off with a bang, until my hamstring injury flared up again. So I was on and off that year. We continued to win, losing just three games all season. My hamstring mended slower than I had hoped, in part because I kept rushing myself and kept re-injuring it. I had to be put on injured reserve, and Nat took my place.

We didn't win the Super Bowl that year, losing to Oakland in the AFC Playoffs on a last-minute touchdown pass by Ken Stabler. I was heartbroken, feeling helpless on injured reserve, because in my heart I knew I could help my team. But that's the breaks of professional sports.

12

Behind the Scenes with the Perfect '72 Dolphins

When I first arrived in Miami after the trade with Buffalo, I realized for the first time that I had to fully grasp the mental aspect of the game. Though I had experienced individual success the previous year in Buffalo, the fact was I came from a 1-13 team. But Shula knew, from coaching against us, what I could do.

Before I got to Miami, I was pretty much scared to death of Shula. His reputation was that of a very tough person, who ran his training camps with an iron fist. You had to be in your best-ever physical condition for camp.

Coach Shula's demeanor was intimidating. You knew what he was thinking from the expression on his face when you did something wrong. So it was worse when he didn't say anything because you could see what he was thinking in his face and his body language. He was so thorough. I had never experienced that before. He and his staff were just so attentive to every detail.

Don Shula set the goal and the path to it.

Shula let his assistant coaches coach, and that was why he was so successful. Several of his assistants went on to become head coaches in the NFL.

Our defense was always in sync, led by defensive coordinator Bill Arnsparger. Our defense played a lot of zone coverage, and we did a great job of disguising it because of our coaches' game plan. Our offensive line coach was Monte Clark, who was outstanding, uniting a talented group of former cast-offs and molding it into one of the greatest lines in league history. Clark went on to become a head coach in Detroit and San Francisco.

My coach—the receivers coach—was Howard Schnellenberger, a real "pipe and slippers" kind of guy. He always had that pipe going. He wasn't a real rah-rah kind of guy, and wasn't that personable. Put a bathrobe on the guy and he would have looked like Hugh Hefner. We'd forget that we had a position coach, until we made a mistake, and Howard pointed it out right away because of his outstanding knowledge of the game.

In short, Coach Shula's confidence in his staff was well founded.

The fact that so many went on to become head coaches shows how he let the coaches show their own talents. I had been with teams where the head coach had to have the final say on everything. That led to a stressful situation where assistant coaches would second-guess themselves.

Shula demanded excellence in every facet of the game. He was a great practice coach, because he knew better than anyone that teams played the way they practiced. He was meticulous with practice. I had a lot of success in Buffalo, but I had survived mostly on talent. I didn't know what professional football was all about until Shula. I made a lot of mistakes initially with the Dolphins, because I was doing things the way I had with Buffalo. I'd even get irked sometimes because I was doing it right—the right way in Buffalo. But that wasn't the right way in Miami.

Playing against the Dolphins, that was one thing—to be on the team was different. I was able to get to know the coaches and players as individuals. That team had several different types of personalities—we had our own cliques—but the same goal. We didn't really hang out together. The atmosphere was very professional and methodical. I learned you didn't have to be extremely close off the field to be successful.

If the head coach is a disciplinarian, the team plays that way. We mirrored Coach Shula that way; we were well organized, physically imposing, disciplined and tough.

The personality of a team mirrors the quarterback as well. Because it is a position that is, by nature, a leadership role. Bob

Griese was our quarterback, and he was the perfect field general. He could manage a game well. I used to walk up next to him to see how tall he was—to see if the "not tall enough" label stuck on me was valid. Griese was only an inch or two taller than I was. We had a lot of similarities. In his early days, Griese was a scrambler, as was I. He had played basketball at Purdue, as had I at Omaha University.

Griese was a great athlete. He was a lot like Shula, very intelligent, quiet but very demanding. Griese could give a scowl if a player did the wrong move, and the player knew right away he needed to do better. Bob always knew what he was doing because he had the mental part of the game down pat. He demanded excellence on every play.

All of the guys on that team were intelligent and had excellent "football smarts" —that was a prerequisite to be on Shula's team. At the same time, most of us were castoffs from other teams.

In fact, our entire offensive line came from other teams; Larry Little, Jim Langer and Bob Kuechenberg came from other teams, yet all became Pro Bowl players in Miami. Little and Langer made the Hall of Fame, and Kuechenberg was announced as a candidate for the Hall in 2002—an overdue honor for a player who was so tough that he played in Super Bowl VIII against the Vikings with a broken arm.

Our tight end was Marv Fleming—quirky Marv—whose previous legacy was playing for Green Bay under Vince Lombardi including the Ice Bowl "Super Bowl."

Marv was a California guy, a big strong man with a soft voice and the stereotypical California demeanor. People thought he wasn't tough enough, but he was. I remember in training camp, Paul Warfield and I were rooming together. Shula and his coaches roomed next door to us at Biscayne College. Marv had been holding out for more money, and was late coming to camp.

Marv was about 6-foot-5 and 240 pounds, and a real ladies' man. He came to camp wearing earring.

"Coach Shula, notice anything different about me?" Marv asked.

"Yes, Marv, one of your earrings is missing," Shula answered.

Larry Little was a special person. He took me under his wing.

We called him "Chicken" because of his fondness for fried chicken. Larry was a Miami native. He knew the city and was very popular, hosting a camp for disadvantaged kids each year. He had come full circle in the NFL, having been cast off by San Diego and then coming to Miami. Larry was a tremendous athlete. He was, in those days, big for a guard, at 266 pounds. He could run, block and was strong. Larry was also very self-confident. He and I hung around together. We made quite a scene, being the bachelors on the team. I met his mother, who basically took me in as another son, and I met his friends. His younger brother, David, ended up playing linebacker for the Pittsburgh Steelers and was one of the better linebackers of his era. Before that, though, David ended up being a younger brother to me, too. When he was younger—in high school—we'd play basketball together.

Larry settled down and with his wife, Rosie, had two wonderful kids, and became a very good football coach. I'm disappointed he hasn't had the opportunity to coach in the NFL.

Another of the lineman on that team was Wayne "Big Sol" Moore, who started at tackle. He was another former basketball player, a gentle giant and quiet family man who could warm a room with his smile. He passed away a few years back of a heart attack. It hurt to lose that wonderful, gentleman.

Earl Morrall was Griese's backup for the 1972 season in Miami. Griese got hurt the same game I pulled my hamstring, so Morrall was thrust into action.

But he was ready for it. He had plenty of big-time experience in Baltimore. He also had the distinction of being the quarterback when Baltimore lost the Super Bowl to the New York Jets and Joe Namath. Shula coached that Baltimore team.

When Shula left Baltimore, the Colts were dismantled. Johnny Unitas would leave for San Diego a year later. So Miami picked up Earl Morrall. You just had to love Earl. He was a throwback before there were throwbacks. He had that 1950 crew cut and a '50s personality. He was a homespun kind of guy. Earl was just the opposite of Griese—gregarious and very personable around the other players, joking around and loose.

"Maaaaa-rlin, come over here," he'd say to me.

When Earl took over after Griese's injury, he guided us through the meat of the season, doing an excellent job. But in our playoff game against Pittsburgh, Morrall was having a tough game. Griese had just come back the previous week from the injury. The Steelers had our number, so Shula put in Griese.

Griese was sharp, but late in the game we still had some ground to make up. We were facing fourth down and long—maybe 12 yards or so—with the ball near midfield. I went over to stand by Shula.

Our punt team got ready, and then the snap came.

And all heck broke loose.

Larry Seiple, our punter, took the snap and then took off running. "What is he doing!" Shula screamed. "What is he doing!"

When Shula saw Larry was going to make the first down, Shula started jumping up and down like a little kid. Larry had seen something no one else had, and he hadn't alerted anyone. But he got the first down, and kept the drive—and our season—alive.

That was the biggest first down of the season for us. And that play kept us undefeated. To this day when I see the Steelers players, all they talk about is that play. When the tragedy happened on Sept. 11, 2001 with the terrorist attacks, I was traveling from a ceremony in Buffalo with the Bills. I ended up getting grounded in Pittsburgh because all planes were grounded—I was actually deplaned that day in Pittsburgh. Frank Lewis, who was also at the Bills ceremony, was also stranded. Frank was a former Steeler as well. So when we got to our hotel, Frank called Larry Brown.

Larry Brown is a former Steeler—who owns a chain of restaurants in Pittsburgh—and still lives there. The three of us spent nearly four days together that week. Time and again, the conversation came back to that play, and this is nearly 30 years after the fact.

Credit the versatile Larry Seiple for that memory. Larry was an all-purpose guy, officially our punter and back up tight end, but also a running back, receiver and even an emergency backup quarterback. I was also an emergency backup quarterback when Griese was hurt, taking some snaps in practice.

Shula wanted to use all the talent of all the players he had, leaving no stone unturned.

Something else I think is interesting looking back is that Shula really did bring some of the personality to Miami that he had in

Baltimore with the Colts. Griese was smart and poised like Unitas. Howard Twilley was like Raymond Berry, a bit slow but tough. He had Lenny Moore with the Colts, a great receiver. Moore was like Warfield in that Moore had been a running back in college, as Warfield had been at Ohio State.

The guys on our line were just like the line he had with Baltimore.

At running back, Baltimore had Alan Ameche, a big tough runner like our Larry Csonka. Baltimore's Tom Matte was like Jim Kiick, multi-talented and a good third down back with good pass-catching skills.

But we also had that array of personalities.

Mercury Morris would test Shula's patience. He had his own way of doing things. Merc was very outgoing, funny and kind of in his own world. He was a fast, tough back but didn't have the best hands for catching passes, certainly not like Kiick in that regard.

Hubert "Hubie" Ginn, Lloyd Mumphord, Charlie Leigh and Mercury—all 5-foot-10 inches—hung out in what was called "the 5-10" Club. I was the only 5-10 guy on the team that didn't hang with them. Merc was the loquacious one.

I've never seen two players as quiet as Curtis Johnson—the only non 5-foot-10 guy in the "5-10 club"—and Charlie Leigh.

Leigh had been a backup in Cleveland. I loved those two guys, but I never heard more than five words from them, combined. Hubie and Mercury made up for that, always talking, teasing and looking for the next prank.

We also had a great guy named Lloyd Mumphord, a very quiet family man. I called him "Mr. Wizard." Lloyd loved to learn about life. He was in the National Guard and would go scuba diving, craw fishing, water skiing and snow skiing—always trying different things, wanting to experience all that life offers. He was called up during the deadly Kent State protest. One year, Lloyd missed part of camp because his stint with the Guard overlapped with the start of training camp. I thought his commitment to serve his country was very admirable.

Lloyd was the third cornerback on the team. He had the talent to start, and was very instrumental in our success. He'd always be in the right place at the right time, delivering big plays—interceptions or blocked kicks. Lloyd named one of his sons after me, Marlin, and I consider that one of the ultimate shows of respect.

I wasn't in any of the cliques—I hung around with a lot of different guys, even white guys like Jim "Mad Dog" Mandich and Jake Scott.

Jake was one of the best safeties in the game. He played with no fear. It's kind of sad that Jake doesn't go to our Miami reunions. Jake had some sort of feud with Coach Shula—I don't know what is it about—but I still miss Jake when we get back together.

Of course we had Butch Cassidy and the Sundance Kid—Larry Csonka and Jim Kiick. To this day, I don't know which one was Cassidy or Sundance as that label came before I arrived in Miami. But they were great players.

Csonka was a lot like Shula, and was from a town in Ohio not far from where Shula grew up. People thought Csonka always led Kiick around. But Kiick was more street-wise, being from New Jersey, so I think Kiick did a lot of the leading around in that duo.

Csonka played college ball at Syracuse. Kiick can trace his rout to the pros to Omaha, Nebraska, at least indirectly. Kiick went to the University of Wyoming, but was a backup to outstanding sophomore Bill Dodd.

If you recall, I mentioned Bill Dodd earlier. He was from Nebraska, and was the Most Valuable Player in the Shrine Bowl as I quarterbacked his North team. But after going to Wyoming, he longed for Omaha. So he transferred after his sophomore year back to Omaha University and played with me, clearing the way for Kiick to start and establish himself as one of the top backs in college football, which of course he used as a springboard to pro football.

"I probably wouldn't have been the starter until my senior year if Bill hadn't left," Kiick told me.

Paul Warfield was probably the greatest receiver in the game—no disrespect to Jerry Rice. If Warfield had played in an offense like Rice did, he would have put up amazing numbers. Warfield played with Jim Brown and Leroy Kelley, two great running backs, in Cleveland, so he didn't have a chance to put up the numbers he could have. And then Warfield came to Miami, where the Dolphins had Larry Csonka, Jim Kiick and Mercury Morris, so he still wasn't

in a pass-oriented offense. But he was the consummate professional. No one could cover Warfield. Just watching Warfield prepare left
me in awe. When I first joined the Dolphins Warfield really took me
under his wing.

I was at practice one day with my back turned, and I heard this
guy counting, "One two, three, four, five, six..."

It was Warfield.

"What are you doing?" I asked him.

"When you line up on the left side, you have a certain amount
of steps, but on the right side it's different," Warfield said. "The way
we set up, it takes you one less step on the right side on a slant pattern, than it does the left side, where it's six steps to get to your spot.
On the right side, it's five steps."

I was just amazed.

With Shula being so precise, we had to be in exactly the right
position. I started counting steps, and sure enough, Paul was correct. By the time we started playing games, getting to the exact
right place was ingrained in our minds.

Warfield was a great blocker. He was mild mannered, but he
delivered the most vicious blocks. Though we were certainly good
friends, we didn't hang out much together because he was married,
very much a family man, and quiet. He and his beautiful wife, Beverly, remain close friends of mine. He led a no frills life, keeping
things simple. He was also a great father.

On the field, our relationship was professional, and very special.
He taught me how to be precise. Really, Warfield was poetry in
motion. There's never been a receiver, in my book, as good as he
was. I take my hat off to Jerry Rice, because he's so talented and
such a hard worker. But I think Warfield could have put up Rice's
numbers if he was in the West Coast offense for his entire career.
When I later had problems with drugs, Paul came all the way across
the country to try and help me. That says a lot about him.

Another receiver—and person—who meant a lot to me, on and
off the field, was Howard Twilley. If you recall, I was brought in
because Dallas had shut down Howard in the Super Bowl with single coverage the year before, 1971, so Dallas could double-cover
Paul Warfield and take him out of the game. Shula brought me in
to solve that problem, and push Howard. Howard also pushed me

as we competed for the starting job all three years I was there. I won the starting job each of the three years, though I was injured and replaced by Howard, roles that would be reversed the next year after he became the starter early in the year before getting hurt. The third year I won the starting job again, but was replaced by Nat Moore.

Though he didn't have a lot of speed—Howard wasn't a catch-and-run receiver like Warfield, or me—he played hard. Howard was a great receiver in his own right. He set records at the University of Tulsa that I believe stand to this day. I used to read all about Howard in magazines when I was in college.

Howard was the kind of player who could get the big catch. We made each other better. He was also a tenacious blocker, the toughest we had in our group. He was the kind of warrior who would just knock your block off. He and Bob Griese were good friends. Larry Seiple also hung out with those two.

Let me tell you about the character of Howard Twilley. When I came out of my drug problems, Howard Twilley was the first one to step up and offer help—that's the kind of man he is. I needed rent for an apartment when I got out of jail—which was a requirement for my teaching job in the school system. Howard and his amazing wife, Julie, discussed my situation together. They decided that since I was just out of jail, and trying to get back on my feet, that they would help me with my rent. They believed in me, and came through for me. That act of kindness, and generosity, shows the kind of character that Howard Twilley has.

We had another receiver, Otto Stowe. He backed up Warfield, and was an up-and-coming receiver from Iowa State. Otto looked like Sly Stone, wanted to be like Sly Stone, and dressed like Sly Stone. He had the same mannerisms, and everything. Remember, that was the era when Sly and the Family Stone were very popular. Otto had a tough time at first, because he brought his girlfriend, Judy. He was black, and she was white. There wasn't much interracial dating at that time, and Miami was in the South—that's not well known or much talked about, but it's true. So interracial dating was a hidden taboo. Yet Otto and Judy got married and have lasted all these years. None of the players raised an eyebrow about them dating back then, but that they survived the societal stares and scrutiny says a lot about who they are as people, and their love for each other.

Another player I really enjoyed was Nick Buoniconti. I used to watch a lot of football when I was in college, and kept up with the AFL and NFL. Buoniconti's name always came up. He was small, maybe 225 pounds, but smart and very aggressive. He was one of the best middle linebackers in the game.

My first game as Denver's quarterback was against Nick. I have to confess he was a big concern. Most of the linebackers suited my style of play—they were big and slower, so I my talent matched up well. But Nick was so quick that I knew he could probably neutralize my scrambling ability. I was so impressed with how he handled himself, and how quickly he covered the ground.

I ended up playing against him when I was in Buffalo as well. To be able to be a teammate of Nick Buoniconti was special. From being foes, we already shared a mutual respect. He embraced me being in Miami right away. He was always a completely classy person. He never let his size determine his success or failure. I was a fan of the "little guys" for a reason, since I was considered small. Nick used his size, or lack thereof, to motivate him. He anchored the "no-name" defense in Miami. He was the focal point when he played for the Patriots, and the Dolphins. Without his leadership, tenacity and intelligence, our defense wouldn't have been as strong.

Another linebacker on that team was Doug Swift, who was the union player representative for the Dolphins. Since I had been the player rep with the Bills, I was the alternate player rep. He was the consummate, ultimate intellectual. He was from Amherst, Massachusetts, and planned to go to medical school. He'd be reading medical books when we'd travel. He dressed like a hippie but he was always studying for his eventual career in medicine. He was one of the smartest guys on the team. He ended up becoming a very fine doctor.

I can't leave the Dolphins without mentioning our kicker, the famous—and infamous—Garo Yepremian. We called him "Keebler," because he reminded everyone of the Nabisco cookie elf. But Garo was very cocky, and he always made the big kick. He was at his best under pressure. Garo was always involved in outside business ventures.

The main man with the financial strings was Joe Robbie. It was a shame he dismantled that team after the 1974 season. We had been within a play of making it back to the conference championship, and I have no doubt we could have made it to the Super Bowl.

What was disappointing was how the team was broken up. When Warfield, Kiick and Csonka signed with the fledgling World Football League, all they wanted was for Robbie to match the salaries they had been offered, which was a mere pittance compared to the salaries of today. All three of those players really wanted to stay. But we all ended up leaving. Those three left for the WFL, Mercury Morris went to San Diego, Jake Scott went to the Redskins, Otto Stowe went to Dallas, Lloyd Mumphord to Baltimore, Hubert Ginn to St. Louis and Marv Fleming retired because he didn't want to play anywhere else.

I had to meet with Robbie after the 1974 season, in 1975, to see if he wanted me back. He didn't, and didn't offer me a contract. A couple of months later, I went home to Omaha to be enshrined in the University of Nebraska at Omaha (formerly Omaha University) Hall of Fame.

And who is there to present the awards?

Joe Robbie.

I had no idea he would be there, and I assume he had no idea I'd be there. He was a respected businessman and had ties to the area, so he was an honored guest. I would have loved to see his face when he arrived and found out I was one of the people that he'd be honoring. Al Caniglia, my coach at Omaha U., knew about the contract squabble and asked me if I wanted someone else to present the award. I said I had no problem with it, because the high road was the best road for everyone involved. Robbie was very cordial that night. But it was ironic to have him there as my praises were announced. I just chalk it up to another twist of fate.

What a great team to be on. We took the field knowing we were going to win. We lost only five games in three years. That was one finely tuned machine. Had we stayed together, we could have been the greatest NFL dynasty ever.

13

A Chance Encounter with Joe Gilliam

Since I hadn't been traded yet in January of 1975, I was working out during the Super Bowl week. The game was in Miami. The Steelers were training at the facility at Biscayne College. When I came out of the locker room, I stopped to watch the practice. There were two practice fields. The Steelers were practicing on one field, and Joe Gilliam, another of the first black quarterbacks to follow me, was on the other, throwing at the goal posts. After beating out two outstanding quarterbacks—Terry Bradshaw and Terry Hanratty—to win the starting job, Joe had guided the team to a record of 4-1-1. But Gilliam was benched in favor of Bradshaw.

Gilliam took offense to that, and distanced himself from the team. I went over and introduced myself, even though I felt funny since practice was going on. But the guys on the team knew who I was—we had to go through the Steelers to get to the Super Bowl the previous year—so I wandered over to Joe.

"I'm Marlin Briscoe," I said, extending my hand.

"Yes, I know," Gilliam said, cordially shaking my hand.

"You know, you have a lot of talent," I said. "I think it's an injustice, what happened to you. But don't let that affect you to the point you're a cancer on the team."

"It's just hard, man," Gilliam said.

I didn't know if he heeded my advice or not. I do know it didn't work out for him in Pittsburgh.

Of the first four black quarterbacks—myself, James Harris, Eldridge Dickey and Joe Gilliam—three of us had substance abuse problems off the field.

Eddie Robinson coached Harris at Grambling, and Robinson was a great developer of talent, but more importantly, he was into honing character and developing life skills. Robinson understood the psychology of the sport, and how it applied to life.

Dickey and Gilliam didn't have that kind of support. They were larger than life in college, and rode that into professional football. So pro ball was a rude awakening for them, and I believe that caught up to them—the lack of discipline to stay away from the dark side in dealing with their disappointment. They were in a league and a society where they were no longer "the man," as they had been on their college campus.

James Harris, on the other hand, had the kind of character and perspective that kept him from going down the wrong path. Harris had a maturity that served him well. He dealt with the incredible disappointment with strong character. The rejection didn't take the toll on him that it did on me. I knew Harris well. I was more outgoing and expressive. Harris had that deep understanding of the big picture, and that incredible perspective.

I had moved past the initial disappointment of what happened in Denver and had made the most of it initially, having a lot of success by going another direction, learning a new position, and excelling. But I never dealt with the feelings that I had from not being able to play the position I coveted. That rejection had to take a deep toll on a human being, especially after we had all succeeded to varying degrees.

We had all performed at quarterback. I had excelled in Denver. Dickey had basically beaten out Ken Stabler, and had stepped aside to switch positions to not rock the boat, and keep a place for himself at a different position. Harris had put up good numbers in Buffalo, and would go onto a good career with a different team. Joe Gilliam beat out Terry Bradshaw, and had gone 4-1-1—not 1-4—so he had done the job. Apparently, Joe was partying too much and had offended the Steelers brass, so they felt like they had to make a change. Plus, Joe had reportedly received death threats and other hate mail, which had to be hard to handle.

Yet all four of us had been told, "You can't cut it," even though we had showed we could. Harris never let that affect him outside of football, and I admire him for it. I've spent a lot of time going over the irony in my mind, that three of the first four of us ended up in such turmoil, and basically left society for substance abuse. I feel like I let down so many people, because my foundation was solid, from my mother and Coach Bob Rose to Coach Al Caniglia. But that support network sort of fell apart as I set out on my own into the new world of professional football.

Joe Gilliam died on Christmas Day, 2000, of an accidental drug overdose—cocaine. He had beaten the cocaine for the previous three years, and even run a football camp at his alma mater, Tennessee State, the year before he died.

"I thought if you played well, you got to play," Gilliam told The (Nashville) Tennessean newspaper in a 1999 interview. "I guess I didn't understand the significance of being a black quarterback at the time."

None of us really understood. I hope that now, everyone does.

As I mentioned, I played in Miami for the 1974 season. At that time, our off days were Monday, and then a half day on Tuesday. I lived next to the Doral Country Club. Paul Warfield was taking golf lessons with a couple of professionals, including Eddie Bush, who had played against Sam Snead, Bobby Jones and Byron Nelson—the top players from that era on the PGA Tour. Paul took me with him to his lessons one day. Though I became a huge golf fanatic, I wasn't into golf at the time, but I lived on the course.

Johnny was giving Paul some lessons. I went over and picked up some clubs, just kind of messing around.

This black man came up behind us, a tall, distinguished looking man. Arthur Ashe was the head tennis teaching professional there, though he lived in California. In 1975, he of course beat Jimmy Connors to win Wimbledon. At the time I met him, Arthur was picking up golf, too. He was the most classy, distinguished diplomatic man I ever met. I had followed—and admired—him throughout my college years. Plus I was a big tennis player. I used playing tennis to stay in shape.

Of course Arthur was well read, so he knew that I had broken the color barrier and been the first black quarterback to start in professional football.

Arthur said he could give me tennis lessons at some point. We never found time for the lessons, but getting to know him was a real treat. He didn't look like a guy who would challenge the system. But he did. And he did it with dignity and class. When he won Wimbledon the next year, I was so proud. He was just such an intelligent, well-spoken man that it was amazing to be in his presence for a long period of time—just an outstanding experience.

After watching Warfield play golf, I eventually picked up the sport, and became somewhat of a golf fanatic. Jackie Gleason had a golf tournament at Doral that I would eventually play in. I got to meet Jackie, and even go to his house. That was such a pleasure. He was divorced from June Taylor, the dancer. In the divorce decree, Jackie got half the house, and she got the other half. They literally lived like that for a while. The guy had a bar in every room, even the bathroom. I had grown up watching Jackie Gleason on TV.

I named my oldest daughter, Angela, after Angela Davis. Back then blacks were being revolutionary, not physically, but mentally and intellectually. Angela Davis was controversial because of her communist connections. When I first joined the Dolphins, Angela Davis had been considered an international fugitive because of her alleged ties to the several revolutionary organizations, including the Black Panthers. She espoused "black power" and the cause of African Americans. She had actually been the subject of a nationwide manhunt—and been on the FBI's 10 Most Wanted list—because of a prison break in California in which four people were killed. Though she wasn't implicated in the escape—the prisoners were African Americans who Davis believed were being wrongly held—the guns were registered in her name, and she was thus implicated and wanted. She would eventually be cleared and start a group called the National Alliance Against Racist and Political Repression, a group that remains active to this day.

During the time that she was sought, I had met an upstart attorney, George Knox. He became the city attorney for Miami eventually. Before that though, he, his wife, Joyce, Ed Poindexter, several others and myself formed a group called the Southern Circle.

We dealt with the Haitian refugee situation. We felt that the Haitians, because they were black, were getting a bad deal trying to get into our country. They were shipped home, whereas other ethic groups were allowed in, carte blanche. We weren't against the other groups coming in, but we thought the Haitians were mistreated. They would risk their lives, often drowning, as the small, often ramshackle boats would sink.

Ed Poindexter, from that Southern Circle group, and I would play chess. He harbored Angela Davis when the world was trying to capture her. When the police searched Ed's place—my apartment was in that same building—I came home and saw all of these FBI and police cars in front of my building. Just four doors down from my place, Angela Davis had lived in Poindexter's place. I never knew that because Ed and I played chess at my place, or at the house of my teammate, Eddie Jenkins, a rookie from Holy Cross— who would go onto be the city attorney for Boston. Eddie ended up being like a little brother to me, tagging along when I'd go places.

The link to Angela Davis didn't end there. In 1975, when I won the Rozelle lawsuit, I went from Miami to St. Louis, San Diego and Detroit, all in one year. When I ended up in Detroit, I became friends with Ben Davis, a cornerback for the Lions, whom I went up against in practice. Ben Davis happened to be the brother of Angela Davis. Ben was one of the nicest guys I ever met, and ended up becoming good friends with Paul Warfield. Ben, of course, supported his sister. I told him how I named my oldest daughter after his sister, and how everything had unfolded in Miami. She was really one of my heroes, especially throughout college.

One week that 1975 season, we went from Detroit to San Francisco for a road game. On Saturday night, I was sitting in my hotel room. It was almost 9:30 p.m., and we had an 11 p.m. curfew. I heard a knock at my door.

"Marlin, I have a fine woman downstairs who wants to meet you," Ben said with a sly smile. I was a bachelor, so I was interested. "She's sitting in a car. Go meet her."

I got dressed—I was already waiting for curfew—and went downstairs. Sure enough, there's the car, and a woman in it. I went to the car and knocked on the door. The woman turned around.

It was Angela Davis.

We talked for a full 90 minutes, right up until I had to be back in my room for curfew. It was one of the most awe-inspiring moments of my life. She was a hugely important figure for young black people, right up there with Malcolm X and Martin Luther King. Meeting her was a beautiful experience.

And yet the link to Angela Davis didn't end there.

My daughter attended San Francisco State before transferring to Cal-Berkley. One of her teachers at San Francisco State ended up being Angela Davis. My daughter went up and told her who she was, and of course Angela Davis remembered

The Lord has blessed me with meeting a lot of people whom I admire. Getting to know them as real people—instead of just how they were portrayed by the media—is a blessing I am grateful for to this day.

14

Rozelle Lawsuit Makes Me a Nomad

In 1975, I had some things I had to work out for my own career. Because of my displeasure with being put on injured reserve—and since we had beaten Rozelle soundly in court—it was time for me to take another direction. Nat Moore was ready to play for the Dolphins, and I had played out my contract.

The league changed in 1975, and it was the end of the Dolphins as we knew it. A fledgling league, the World Football league, needed credibility, which meant top-of-the-line players. They signed Jim Kiick, Paul Warfield and Larry Csonka, three of our premier players. Their contracts had been up with Miami, so they were out of the Dolphins' fold. Joe Robbie and the Dolphins management decided to start from scratch. A lot of players, like me—veterans without contracts—were no longer in the plans. Marv Fleming, Hubert Ginn, Lloyd Mumphord and Mercury Morris were all let go. We had a great run, losing only five games in three years, something no other team has done. But that run was over as the team was gutted and the team has never won a Super Bowl since.

I, too, was headed for a new home, but where? Surely, there must be a home for a guy who had played very well and was just three years removed from being traded for a first-round draft pick.

And talk about timing: We won our judgment in the Rozelle lawsuit in 1975, some four years after we filed.

Both the federal court and the court of appeals wrote that the restrictions provided with the Rozelle Rule violated anti-trust laws. The courts agreed that the owners' claims that the best competitive balance would be destroyed because players would leave their teams for the most lucrative owners and the best cities in which to play were unfounded. By extinguishing the Rozelle Rule, the court said the implications of its ruling would affect all teams equally. The court added that if there was any effect on the competitive level of the league, the owners and Rozelle still should have used less restrictive measures.

The win took a toll on Mackey, and shows how revered Rozelle was by the electors of the Hall of Fame, because Mackey was passed over for induction to the Hall until his 15th—and final—year of eligibility. That was a much belated honor to the man who made tight end into the position it is today, and it was all because he had the courage to stand up for his right to earn a fair living. I still see Mackey at golf tournaments and other events. I saw him in 2001 at a golf tournament at Lake Tahoe, and we sat around the fire one night and talked about the lawsuit and everything that came out of it.

At that point, I was faced with testing the free agent market with the label of beating Rozelle in court on my forehead. Each of us who remained on the suit were pushed out, some sooner than others. Some, liked Mackey, were ostracized by the institution of the NFL itself by such measures as the Hall of Fame treatment. Others lost paychecks, jobs—their livelihoods.

That we would eventually win the Rozelle lawsuit—and be awarded damages, with more to follow in another case—opened up the doors to free agency. The Mackey suit over the Rozelle Rule spawned a class action suit on similar grounds by Kermit Alexander, and that was more costly to the owners, in the $22 million range. The union did give back some of those concessions in the 1977 collective bargaining agreement, but progress is often two steps forward, and one back.

Don't get me wrong: With the Rozelle Rule lawsuit, I wasn't hoping we'd get players the $15 million a year they are getting now (although if an owner or general manager is offering the money, I have no problem with a player signing to accept it—wouldn't you?), or even $1 million a year. In fact, it wasn't so much about salaries as it was having the right to leave if your contract was up or at least get a fair-market salary.

My career took a spiral in terms of stability, something I attribute to the Rozelle lawsuit. I would be traded to four different teams within the course of the 1975 training camp and season. Yet, I would start for every one of those teams, just as I had started for Buffalo and Miami as well.

I was proud of the changes the lawsuit brought for players. It provided a better balance as it altered the financial landscape of the league, and more importantly, gave players some input and wrested control out of the hands of the owners and their general managers and coaches, who made the football decisions. Player salaries climbed significantly—if not dramatically—and almost instantly after the Rozelle judgment was issued by the courts.

So I remain proud to have been a part of that suit, even though it would end my career prematurely.

I went from the Dolphins to the St. Louis Cardinals, and then to the San Diego Chargers, before I was sent to the Detroit Lions to finish out the season. Certainly, that comes with the business, and professional sports were a business. I put my full effort into making the best of it. I decided I would not let it break me, that I'd roll with the punches and take care of business.

I had a good training camp in St. Louis, with Jim Hart at quarterback and Olympic-level sprinter Mel Gray on the other side at receiver. Earl Thomas was a bigger receiver who was accomplished, but didn't move as well. I was in a good situation because Coach Don Coryell, who would eventually go to San Diego and revolutionize the passing game, was the coach for the Cardinals. But the Busch family was pretty frugal. I had to pay my own moving expenses. During camp, I was traded to San Diego.

San Diego's coach was Tommy Prothro who had been a renowned college coach. Dan Fouts was in his second year at quarterback. The Chargers of that year reminded me of the Bills from 1969 to 1971, with a lot of talent, but lacking the structure and organization that Miami had. We started the season 0-3, and Prothro decided to scrap the season and get rid of a lot of the veteran players. I was waived, and picked up by Detroit. I ended up with the Lions, and had a very good year, starting for them.

The Lions were my first NFC team after playing my eight years in the AFC, which had evolved from the AFL. The quarterback for the Lions was Greg Landry, the first-team small college all-American the year I was second team as a college senior at Omaha University. Greg told me, "I always thought you were white," and we laughed about that. Certainly, that wasn't the first time I had heard that comment—or the one I heard the most after my senior year at Omaha U., "I didn't know you were black." Greg was a very educated, intelligent guy—a nice person—and very good quarterback.

In 1976, I was traded during training camp to the New England Patriots. The coach was Chuck Fairbanks, who had been at Oklahoma and had some exciting games against Nebraska, so I knew of him. I ended up being the starter. New England had been 11-3 the year before, and we went 11-3 again.

We would have gone to the Super Bowl if it weren't for a blown call in the playoffs in the last second that gave the Oakland Raiders another play, one they turned into a touchdown pass from Ken Stabler to Fred Biletnikoff. That was a bitter pill to swallow, because we had beaten the Raiders 54-3 earlier in the season. But that's sports—sometimes the calls go for you, and sometimes against you. There are a lot of things you can control, and many you can't. Handling those are valuable life lessons as well, as far as learning to roll with the punches and never giving up.

I want people to understand that unequivocally. The irony is though, that, like all aspects of society, drugs were always around, even from the time I started in the league. At first, the drug of choice for players was alcohol. It was the macho thing to do, I guess, to drink liquor or beer. From there, I saw the stair stepping up the substance ladder—which leads to a downward spiral. In the early 1970s, marijuana became more prevalent. By 1973, there was a lot of cocaine. The NFL was just a microcosm of society.

When free-basing cocaine and heroin entered the picture, it started costing players their careers, and occasionally their lives. I remember a famous linebacker who was a big drinker, even before and during games. He'd spike his Gatorade with vodka, and was just a raging terror on the field. I knew what he was doing—we all knew. Yet he played so well that no one questioned him, even though he was half drunk the whole time. And I saw players who smoked marijuana before games. I suppose people in society do it at work as well. As a player, I was serious about my game, and performing the best I could. So I played and conducted myself accordingly. The only reason I'm making the point so passionately right now is because of my post-career drug problem. So I want to set the record straight that I wasn't doing that as a player.

After the 1976 season ended, I was contemplating playing one more year, bringing my career to 10 years, meaning 1977 would be my final in the league. I had already outlasted anyone's prediction.

Ray Perkins, who would go on to become a successful head coach, was our receivers coach in New England. Ray and Fairbanks liked the drills that I had brought to the team, drills that Paul Warfield and I had devised in Miami to improve footwork. I worked with Darryl Stingley, who would end up getting paralyzed on a hit by Raider Jack Tatum, and talented tight end Russ Francis. Perkins let me teach the drills. We had a young receiver named Stanley Morgan who was brought in and groomed to succeed me, just as Nat Moore had done in Miami. At that point, I was 31 years old.

I ended up having one of my best training camps ever. At the last cut, I wasn't among the names. I was so happy. Two other receivers were cut. I went out to celebrate beating the odds and earning a spot on the team.

The next morning, the tide changed. I was cut, and they had re-signed the two players they had cut the previous day to keep me. I had been smart though, getting my first and only guaranteed contract by negotiation, so I did have some money coming in. Plus I had bought a house in Los Angeles—which had become my off-season adopted hometown—and rented it out.

"That's tough," I thought when I was found out I was cut. "I didn't make it 10 years, but I did make it nine. I did everything expected of me, and even more."

I don't think that's an exaggeration whatsoever. And I didn't feel like I had anything else to prove. There was no question my options were limited because of the Rozelle suit. And I was, quite frankly, tired of fighting for what I thought I deserved. To be honest, I probably was at the tail end of my career, though under the right circumstances I had it in me physically to play another two or three years. But my heart wasn't in pursuing it any longer. I walked away from the game with my head held high, and no regrets.

So in 1977, I went back to Los Angeles, ready to finally live my life without being accountable to anyone for my time and what I did each day. In pro ball, there are so many things that were out of my control. Even when I was in the off-season, I still had to work or go to school or make appearances, so there was still that responsibility even though we weren't in season.

That would change. For the first time since I could remember, I had to be responsible.

I thought I was very well prepared for retirement from pro football. I had my college degree and had made some very good friends.

Yet all of the sudden, I had nothing to do. I never realized how difficult the transition would be. I had played a professional sport at the highest level, and had the adoration of thousands of fans. I had teammates who had been my family. Regardless of the post-career preparation an athlete has—especially those who reach the pinnacle—it's hard to give it all up.

I needed new challenges. I missed the camaraderie of the guys. I missed the smell of the grass. Heck, I missed the smell of liniment in the locker room! The talks we had among ourselves as players were great memories, but memories that would be made no more. The emotion of winning and losing was like a drug in itself.

Since my house was rented out when I left for New England's training camp, I went back to L.A.

James Harris had resurrected his career with the Rams but was still facing down one racial injustice after the other. He had taken the team to the playoffs the two previous years and was the team's most valuable player. Yet he was demoted, and another chapter was added to the black quarterback saga. James was traded to San Diego, so he let me live in his L.A. house, which was next door to my house, which was rented out until the end of the year.

I settled in, but it was unsettling. I began to lose my focus. Quickly, the foundation that had been built for me in the Omaha projects, in school, at church, at home and then in college was slipping away. I started hanging out with some very unsavory people.

No longer did I have a fraction of the 24/7 discipline that I had possessed as a professional athlete. I was in a big house with a swimming pool, and had a Mercedes. I had a job as a broker in a Century City office, so I was among the elite in a very ritzy area. So in that regard, I was certainly set for a successful transition to the "real world" and had plenty of challenges with my new career.

The "unsavory" people I met were very successful on the surface—money, high-paying jobs, and running in elite social circles. I had never really run in a social circle because—even though I was well traveled in my career—I never had a steady dose of any one city's lifestyle. Sports were my lifestyle. I was just a young man from the Midwest.

I started dating a woman and had a wonderful child with her. We had corresponded as my career wound down, and I thought we'd make a good match. We didn't. We were oil and water, just the perfectly wrong fit.

I started using drugs on a recreational basis. I wasn't strung out at that point, but I was doing drugs—I was having a good time.

Or so I thought.

I was lying in bed after an all-night party, a common occurrence. I had left the radio on at James' house. At 3:30 a.m., the radio caught my attention. I started to roll over to turn it off. The newscast had started, and the broadcaster was saying, "a gunman in Omaha, Nebraska, has gone berserk."

Wow, I thought to myself, that's my hometown.

"The gunman has killed a police officer and wounded another person," he said. "The name of the gunman, according to authorities, is Ulysses S. Cribbs, age 32."

The breath left my body. I felt like I had been punched in the head.

"Just a dream," I said, my head hitting the pillow, "just a really bad dream."

The news continued, and I realized it wasn't a bad dream.

"It's real!" I cried out. "This has really happened!"

I called my mother. I could tell she had been sound asleep, but it was 5:30 a.m. in Omaha, so she would be getting up soon.

"Did you hear about the murder?" I asked breathlessly.

"Yes, horrible," she said. "They don't know who did it yet."

"No, that's the thing, Mom, they do know," I said. "It's Butch!"

"Butch Cribbs?" she said. "Heavens, no!"

Indeed, my best friend in life had snapped. People never realized that Butch was on the edge. I knew he was when he left

Omaha University to go into the service. He was having some emotional problems. He would confide in me some of the different things going through his mind. I knew he was having some severe problems, but I had no idea it would lead to something like that. That was before pop-psychology was huge and they had a drug for everything.

It had been Butch Cribbs who killed the officer. I had to go back to Omaha eventually to testify. I testified about his mental state, growing up together and so on. I wasn't there to excuse or justify what he had done. I was there to tell what I knew about a friend I loved like a brother. I wasn't trying to get him out of his debt to society. Rather, I was trying to make sure society gave Butch the debt that he deserved. That didn't endear me to a lot of people in Omaha who were related to the victims. I had wanted to go back home, but my decision to testify would hamper me.

Yet I had always been a positive citizen, never went to juvenile hall, never got in trouble—my record was exemplary. I was always available for public appearances to lend a hand, and I had sent 10 Omaha kids to college through a foundation I set up—I did it out of my heart, before it was a fashionable public relations move for athletes to set up foundations, sometimes as a tax write-off.

By testifying, I was cast out of the group I needed to belong to in order to get back to Omaha. I was estranged from the so-called shot callers. It would later lead to me losing my two Super Bowl rings—though I have no one else to blame—as I had pawned them during my years of drug abuse.

The bigger issue at the time, though, was the loss of life. That of the victim and the tragic, senseless wounding of his wife—who was shot, but survived—and that of Butch Cribbs. Losing him was heart-breaking and gut-wrenching. I wish we could have helped him because that would have saved the victims and their families.

I went back to L.A. and the trappings of success were ready to let me paint myself into a corner. Everyone loves a winner, and because of my NFL career and the Super Bowls, I was a winner. I started using cocaine more often and smoking marijuana. Initially, I still wasn't what could be considered a junkie. I'd rationalize it in my mind because a lot of people I worked with snorted cocaine—some would do it on lunch breaks. I didn't realize I was developing

a serious problem, one that would take away everything I loved—
everything I had.

I had a beautiful daughter, Angela, from a relationship in 1972
previous to Nikki, who gave birth to our daughter Rebecca in 1979,
making her eight years younger than Angela. My marriage continued to go downhill.

Soon thereafter, I was introduced to free-basing cocaine, which,
again, started out recreationally. But my addiction was becoming
more and more entrenched. I could sense things were getting out
of control. I was not prepared for—and didn't know—what drugs
could do to a person.

My use climbed and climbed. I lost sight of the things that
made me proud, such as being a father, as I sunk further into the
abyss that is drugs. I had survived two years going to work, selling
municipal bonds, and raising a family, my wife also had a daughter
from a previous relationship. So it appeared from the outside that I
had it all. In reality, I had nothing, because I didn't have a handle
on a drug problem that was consuming my life—every day, every
minute, every dollar and every ounce of my attention.

The light in my life was growing dim. And dimmer. Soon, there
was mostly darkness.

And then, complete darkness.

15

The Darkness of Drugs

I never sold drugs. Unlike a lot of other addicts, I could never afflict my addiction on someone else. I still had a little pride, as much as I could have with drugs overwhelming me.

My cocaine addiction was ironic because to this day, I've only been drunk twice. Both those times were in college, and I got drunk only because my fraternity made me do shots of rum and coke in an initiation ritual. I threw up. It was the worse feeling. I promised myself I'd never again get drunk. And I haven't.

In the NFL, I drank plenty of beer. Especially in Miami, the hottest and most humid NFL city. You lose a lot of fluid playing football in that climate. The heat coming off the Astroturf of the Orange Bowl made it 15 degrees hotter for us on the field. Whenever I'd play in Miami when I was with other teams, my muscles would cramp. But when I played for Miami, Shula had this little ritual to prevent us from cramping in games. On Saturday nights before games, he'd put on what he called a "Burger Bust"—he'd grill up cheeseburgers and he'd have this big vat of beer for us to drink. Beer, he said, would help our bodies maintain electrolytes and prevent us from cramping so much. So we would drink lots of beer the nights before games, even the guys who didn't drink much, like me. It seemed to work.

Beer had never been a problem. Rum and coke, and other forms of alcohol, had never been a problem. Then I tried the other kind of coke.

I trace my descent into drugs to my final four years in the NFL. That's when this straight-laced kid from Omaha started smoking pot. I'd do it with teammates after games, never before–though I saw players smoke pot before games and play well. I even saw guys high on cocaine play well. There was no drug testing back then. Among players, there was a code of silence about alcohol and drugs. I stayed away from cocaine because I knew it was bad, not because I was afraid my coach or the league would find out. I didn't want to take away my control on the football field. I had this warrior mentality.

We didn't make that much money in the NFL back then. My first year's contract was for $10,000. By my last year, I was making $100,000. But I had invested well. Each off-season, I either went to school or I worked. By the time I retired, I was worth close to a million dollars. I had a house with a pool in an upscale neighborhood of L.A. I owned part of a wine vineyard. I had an acre and a half of land up in a place called Bear Valley outside of L.A., right across the valley from the chalet of Carol Rosenbloom, then-owner of the Rams. I had more land than he did. The actor Chuck Connors, TV's "Rifleman," owned a piece of land nearby, too.

At first, I got into cocaine because it was social thing to do. I'd go play basketball or tennis and it was, "Hey, you want to toot (snort cocaine)?"

I partied with other football and basketball players and with doctors and lawyers. At first, everyone I partied with had property and position. Over my lunch breaks at work, my co-workers and I would sit in our luxury cars and snort coke. We were blacks who had beaten the odds. We called ourselves "the black Gatsbys." We got cocky. We got high. Many of us in that crowd later crashed.

I also moved in the Hollywood crowd. I belonged because of my football status—everything in L.A. is about status and name. Pro athletes were popular in that crowd. Actors wanted to hang with the pro athlete, and pro athletes wanted to hang with actors. The two have a lot in common. Both perform for the masses. Both are entertainers. And my friendship with O.J. Simpson, an aspiring actor at the time, opened even more doors.

As a kid, I had worshipped Steve McQueen. I liked his toughness. But I also liked the sensitive side he clearly had. O.J. and I would always talk about movies. He'd talk about the career he wanted as an actor. I'd always talk about Steve McQueen.

"You want to play Liar's Poker?" O.J. asked me one night at a party in Beverly Hills.

"Sure," I said, "if you're willing to lose."

We walked upstairs, and some guys made room for us at the table. O.J. and I sat down and kept laughing and joking with each other. Another guy at the table, a small guy, was sitting with his back to us, his chair turned away. After a few minutes, he turned around to face us.

"Are you going to play, or are you going to B.S. all night?" the man said. He was Steve McQueen.

I almost dropped dead. I couldn't talk. O.J. was sitting there laughing his guts out at me. He had orchestrated the whole scene.

McQueen was just a regular, down-to earth guy. He was a big football fan. He knew everything about me. We all played poker and talked football for hours. I think I lost about $200 that night because I couldn't concentrate.

I ended up becoming good friends with Jim Brown, probably the greatest running back in pro football history. One day, O.J., Al Cowlings and I went up to Jim's place. Elliott Gould and some other stars were there, and we got a game of three-on-three basketball going. Jim ran O.J. into the garage, hard.

We started up playing again after O.J. shook it off. It was no secret that Jim Brown didn't like O.J., be it for O.J.'s demeanor, career or just because O.J. was O.J. Well, on the next play, O.J. went up for his trademark ugly hookshot. Jim ran him into the garage again and even harder this time. Obviously, it wasn't an accident.

"Time to go," I said, shaking hands with Jim and hustling O.J. out of there.

Jim Brown and I are still friends, and were really good friends back then. We would play tennis several days a week in sweltering heat. Jim didn't have the classic tennis stroke, but he could always get to the ball. And he always made a shot, just slicing and dicing his way to winning games. Since I hadn't been playing as long as Jim had, I had more of a learning curve. So I kept improving, and eventually, I started beating him. Big Jim Brown didn't like that too much. My shots that had been out were suddenly in. He's quite a competitor to this day, and I still enjoy his company immensely.

I had a lot of fun those first years away from football. Too much fun. My bank account was big. My head was big. Disco was big. I loved to dance. I thought the music would never stop. My nickname then was "Disco Briscoe."

In those days, drugs were everywhere. So were the women. And I wanted every beautiful woman I saw. Actresses and models.

One day in my house, a beautiful woman taught me how to free-base cocaine. I had just come home from work at the brokerage firm. She was sitting there on my couch.

"Smoke this," she said, holding out a "toker two," the chic free-basing pipe of that time. She had just cooked the coke on my kitchen stove.

I let my guard down. I smoked it. I walked toward my bedroom to change out of my dark blue Brooks Brothers suit and into some slacks and sandals. Before I got to my bedroom, it hit me. Bam! Euphoria swept over me. I didn't know it at the time, but I'd just tried my first hard-core drug.

"What *was* that?" I asked, stunned. I went back for some more.

I was hooked. I wanted that euphoria again. That's what the drug thing is all about—you're always trying to find more drugs to get that that same initial feeling. That euphoria. You wake up in the morning, and you take another hit. You spend all your money, time and energy chasing it. But you never recapture it.

Drugs became my life, though I couldn't admit it.

In 1978, Chuck Fairbanks, who had been my coach at New England Patriots, defected to take the head-coaching job at the University of Colorado. He called me up and asked if I'd be an assistant coach for him at Colorado. My last year at New England, I had basically been a player-coach for Fairbanks, helping the receivers, most notably Stanley Morgan, who had developed into a Pro Bowl receiver.

Because I had coached Stanley Morgan to basically step into my shoes, I guess Fairbanks saw something in me as a potential coach. He saw that I was unselfish. He saw I was a good teacher. But by the time Fairbanks asked me to be an assistant, I was a stockbroker. I was making good money with the potential to make a whole lot more. I was married with a new baby, a new stepdaughter and a mortgage.

One day I got a call at work from "Sugar Bear" Hamilton, the New England defensive star who was called for the bogus roughing the passer against Oakland—that blown call cost our Patriots team a shot at the Super Bowl. Hamilton was playing in the Pro Bowl that year, and Chuck Fairbanks was going to be the head coach. But not for long, as he had already accepted the Colorado job.

"Coach Fairbanks wants to talk to you," Sugar Bear said, giving me Coach Fairbanks' phone number.

I thanked Sugar Bear—it's always good to hear from him—and called Fairbanks.

"You're the first coach I want to hire," Fairbanks told me over the phone.

I thought that was a heck of an honor. I mulled the offer over. Fairbanks explained that Continental Airlines had a deal with Colorado. With the assistant coaching job, I also would be employed by Continental as a manager-in-training during the off-season to supplement the paltry money I'd make as an assistant.

My wife and I discussed it. It seemed like a good situation for us. Continental would fly my wife and the girls back and forth for free each weekend. And, more than anything, for me, it seemed like a good opportunity to extract myself from the L.A. drug scene.

I soon learned that you can't run away from addiction. It follows you. It finds you. Colorado was a party school. There were more drugs in Boulder than in L.A. Instead of getting away from drugs, I sank further into drugs.

Coaching is very demanding. You work from 7 in the morning until 11 at night. At first, I didn't have time to find drugs. Then I became friends with a guy who lived just below me in my Boulder apartment building. He was a real nice college student studying law. His girlfriend, coincidentally, had grown up just three doors down from my house in L.A. Turns out, my new friend was a cocaine dealer.

"Do you toot?" he asked one day.

Just like that, I was back in it nose-deep. I even taught my new friend and his girlfriend how to free-base. Now, all the sudden, it was downstairs and available for me all the time. I was coaching, going to practice, then going home and getting high.

At this point, I started to realize that I was in trouble. I cared about myself. I always tried to keep a job and a roof over my head. I began trying to recapture the old me. But drugs kept winning. My life was spiraling downward.

Fairbanks never noticed my drug problem. He wanted me to come back the next year. But then Continental filed for bankruptcy. The CEO committed suicide. So when I came back from Colorado to L.A. to start work at Continental in the off-season, there was no manager-in-training job waiting for me as promised. There was no extra money. My finances became strained. So did my marriage.

On paper, my decision to go to Colorado had looked good. But it turned into a real nightmare. And to top it off, one weekend while my wife was visiting me in Boulder, a fish tank at my house in L.A. caught fire and did a lot of damage to my den.

After Colorado, I was a mess. My drug use escalated. I still had assets. But I was liquidating them for drugs. I even sold my Mercedes. I didn't know what my future held in terms of my working career. In order to get me back for another year, Colorado had to set me up in another off-season situation. But I didn't want to take a chance on the same thing happening.

And I was trying to mend fences in my marriage. We had been married only a year. The distance that year in Colorado had been difficult. When Fairbanks tried to get me to come back, I said no. He called me several times. Sometimes when he'd call, I was so high I couldn't understand him.

I started staying home, getting high. People came over to my house to free-base. Friends. Strangers. I didn't care who came to party. One time, a plumber came over to fix my leaky pipe in the bathroom. We got to talking. He found out I liked to free-base.

"I'll be back in about 30 minutes," he said, then drove off in his van.

The plumber also was a drug dealer. He returned with all sorts of coke, and we free-based the rest of the day.

With free-basing, you can smoke it, but then put it down and go about your life. It was more of a party drug. It is not as addictive as crack or other hard-core drugs. It was safer because you knew what was in it and because you did it yourself in your home. You weren't under a microscope.

But free-basing is insidious because once you use it, you can easily end up on crack. "Crack" is the smoked form of cocaine that you get on the street. It's not pure. It's not safe. You don't know what's in it. With crack, the dope dealers usually add in speed or LSD or anything that they think will keep you crazy and coming back for more.

The red flag went up in 1981 among my friends and ex-teammates. That is when I started borrowing money from them. James Harris was one of the first to know. My house with the pool was right next to his house with a pool, and I'd knock on his door at odd hours of the day and ask to borrow money.

"Have 100 bucks?" I'd ask. "I can't get to my money right now."

James kept wondering why I needed money. Soon, he figured it out.

I got divorced in 1982. That devastated me. That was the first time I had failed at anything important. I traded my house for another house, a smaller one in a less desirable neighborhood. I just didn't care. It was nuts. And I couldn't help myself.

When I hocked my two Super Bowl rings to a Hollywood pawnshop, word got back to Miami. Paul Warfield heard about it and flew all the way out to L.A. to help me. That was right before my divorce. One day, my soon-to-be ex-wife called and asked me to come over. She didn't say why. I opened the door and there sitting in the living room was Paul.

"I came out here because I'm concerned about your health," he said. "What's happening with you?"

Paul didn't preach to me. He just wanted to find out if I was OK. For him to show that kind of love really touched me. But I still was in denial, especially with Paul, because I respected and loved him so much. He had been my mentor. We were two receivers on that 17-0 team. Our talents had fed off of each other. He had taught me a lot. I just couldn't admit to him that I was an addict.

About that time I borrowed money from my good friend and former Miami teammate Larry Little, another Hall of Famer. I needed help to pay my mortgage. My friends also helped me get my rings out of hock—for the time being, at least.

My downward spiral was a shock to James, Paul, Larry and all of my other ex-teammates. Not only had I been one of the top players on all the teams I'd played on, I also had been voted on by my Miami teammates to be their alternate player representative—the person they wanted to represent them in labor disputes.

So seeing this responsible person go 180 degrees the other way was painful for my ex-teammates. I was a wreck. My real friends from Omaha and the guys I played ball with, stood by me. I hated to hurt them.

Johnny Alexander, who played on that basketball team in Omaha with me when I replaced Jody Sinclair, had moved to Los Angeles and owned a children's shoe shop in Inglewood. He always supported me. He was the one person—the lone one out of everyone—with whom I always stayed in contact.

He knew me so well. One time I was sleeping on a park bench, a newspaper covering me, even my face, and Johnny drove by in his car. Yet he recognized me, and took me out for a nice breakfast. He always cared for me like a family member, unconditionally. When a person is going through drug abuse, he can feel ostracized by those who love him. Even though they are trying to help, the drug user pushes them away because he feels like he is constantly being judged by them, and contact is often lost. That was the case with me, but Johnny was always there.

I ended up living with him when he and his wife separated. He had an alcohol problem, and I tried to help him with that just as he tried to help me with my drug problem. I don't know that we ever really helped each other with our problems, but having that kind of kinship surely helped both of us. We never lost touch.

In August of 2000, I was so excited to talk to him. I let him know that I had just received the deal to write this book, and he shared in the excitement. He called me a couple of days later. I got the message at 8:25 p.m. and picked up the phone to call him. I realized that I had other things to do that night, so I put the phone down, and decided to call him in the coming days. I chose instead to get everything else I had to do organized. I wish I hadn't made that choice. When I did call three days later, I was told he had just passed away suddenly of a massive heart attack. Man, I wish I had called.

16

Kidnapped by Gang-bangers

Guys like Larry Little, Paul Warfield and Johnny Alexander were my real friends. But in the drug world, I had no real friends. I just thought I did.

One time, a drug "friend" almost got me killed. He said that he had a connection to buy cocaine. I didn't know at the time that it was coming from a gang. He told me to write a $1,500 check to buy the drugs because the gang people knew who I was and would take a check. He promised to pay his half to me the next day. But he never paid. My check bounced. He was gone.

The gang people found him before I could. To get the heat off himself, he told them I had written the bad check. He knew where I was, which was in a drug house. I was standing there getting high when he walked in with these three thugs and pointed at me. The thugs, members of the Crips gang, dragged me out and threw me in a car. They literally kidnapped me.

"You wrote a check," one thug said. "You need to make it good or else we're going to do something to you."

They tied my hands behind my back and blindfolded me, then drove me to three or four different gang hideouts. This ordeal began on a Friday night and lasted the whole weekend. When they kidnapped me, I told them I had a check with which I could pay my debts. It was for $7,000. But I had left it over at a friend's house. I was going to cash that check that Monday. I didn't want that check on me because I was afraid someone in the crack house might steal it.

"You'd better have it, or you're dead."

I knew those thugs wouldn't kill me until they got the money. I knew I had the money. So I wasn't afraid. But the friend who had turned me in didn't know I had this other check. He thought they were just going to kill me. Yet he had led them to me anyway, set me up, to keep them from killing him.

Throughout that hellish weekend, my kidnappers, who smoked crack the whole time, kept trying to scare me just for the fun of it. They held a torch they were using to light their crack pipes up to my face. They threatened to burn me.

They put a gun to my head and clicked it. No bullet.

I knew they couldn't kill me because they didn't have their money yet. But when they put that gun to my head, I did think, "This is it."

For the first time in long time, I wasn't high. My heart pounded. My thoughts raced in the darkness behind the blindfold. I thought about my mom—how she hadn't raised me to end up like this. I thought about how I was about to lose my life because of my addiction.

That Sunday, we went over to my friend's house in Inglewood and I retrieved the check. On Monday morning, we went downtown to the bank. A couple of the thugs went in with me, pretending to be my brothers. Another one posted himself outside the door so I wouldn't run. But instead of drawing all the cash out from that $7,000 check, I got out only what I needed to pay off the drug debt. I got the rest of it in a cashier's check so the thugs couldn't get it.

When I got back in the car, I gave them the money owed. One of them put a crack torch to my face again.

"Now," he said, "give me the rest of it."

When they found out that the rest of the money was in a cashier's check, they got real angry. We were on the freeway heading toward San Diego. I knew I had to get out. Fast. Now that they had the money I owed, they could just take me somewhere and shoot me.

The car slowed as it turned a curve. I jumped out, right in the middle of traffic. I ran until I lost them and hid. Then I walked miles to get back home, stopping first at James Harris' house.

The friend who had betrayed me had done a lot of other people wrong, too. He got run out of town. Last I heard, he'd been shot, dead, in another drug deal.

After I had lost all my money and couldn't buy my own pure cocaine that's when I turned to crack. The first time I used crack was after I lost my second house. I moved to an apartment in a place in L.A. called "the Jungle." Back in the '50s and '60s, the Jungle was an upscale row of apartments with pools and huge palm trees—that's how it got its name. By the time I moved to the Jungle, it was seedy. But then, so was I.

I bought my first crack in the alley behind my apartment. I slipped $20 to a man through a slit in a door. Bam! It hit me. I walked back to my apartment in a stupor. I didn't know what was going on. My living room was spinning. My kitchen table kept moving from one side of the room to the other. I was hallucinating. Later, I found out that the drug dealer had mixed in some LSD. I was a product of the '60s, but during that decade of experimentation, not once did I try LSD.

I think back on that day a lot. That first puff of crack was a turning point. But, really, my descent into drugs began the first time I chose to smoke pot. I regret that decision the most. You start one drug; it's easy to go to another, then another, then another. I always thought that I was strong enough to resist drugs. I always thought nothing could keep me down.

Football had given me a false self-image, a feeling of invincibility. But when I got out of ball and found myself in the real world, it was a different world. Maybe I was not really ready to leave sports when I did. Maybe I still wanted the adulation of being a pro football player. The applause. I could have played a few more years. Teams were calling me. But I had said that I wasn't going back. But maybe if I still had been able to keep my football mentality a few more years, that warrior mentality, I wouldn't have gotten into drugs.

People think that only weak people do drugs. But I wasn't weak. Drugs made me weak. Until I got away from them, and I thank God that I did, I was pitiful.

When you're in the drug world, every day, every drug sale, can quickly turn into a Hollywood drama. Though usually it's one without a happy ending.

In 1985, I was teaching math and science at Sun Valley Junior High in Los Angeles. I was living a double life. This is at the point in my descent when I still could project a clean-cut image during the day, even though I was looking for drugs at night. During this time, I became friends with another addict whose nickname was "Baby Brother." He was an outcast in his family. I felt sorry for him, so I always treated him fairly. If Baby Brother didn't have food, I'd share mine. If he didn't have drugs, I'd share mine. I had a car at that time. He didn't. So I'd drive him around with me to look for dealers.

One night, we both were out of drugs. He said he had $20. He said he wanted to go in this really dangerous area of L.A. and buy drugs. We went there and pulled into a dark cul-de-sac where we saw some dealers. I drove to the end of the cul-de-sac.

"Don't stop here," Baby Brother said. "Let's do the sale back where we came in."

I couldn't figure out why he said that. But I made a U-turn in my little Toyota and drove back to the entrance of the cul-de-sac. I pulled up next to a drug dealer and rolled down my window.

"How much do you need?" he asked.

"A dove," said Baby Brother. A "dove" is a street word for 20 dollars worth of crack.

My friend handed me a folded up $20 bill, and I handed it to the brother on the corner. He handed me the crack.

"Let's get out of here," Baby Brother said after I had driven about five yards away.

"What do you mean?" I asked, chills going up my spine.

"Hey, man, let's go. We got to get out of here!"

I accelerated and turned left so fast my wheels went off the ground, just like in a gangster movie. I heard the drug dealer yell something. I ducked just as I heard the gunfire. Pow. Pow. Pow. The back window shattered. A bullet whizzed over my body, which was all but lying flat on the front seat.

When we got back to my apartment, I inspected my car. The bullet that had shot out the back window also had gone through the engine. Then I saw another bullet hole, one on the driver's side door. If I hadn't ducked when I did, I realized I would have been shot twice. The first bullet would have hit me in the head. The second bullet would have pierced my heart.

"What the heck happened back there?" I demanded.

My friend confessed that the $20 bill had been only half of a $20 bill. He had ripped the bill in half to make the drug money go farther, then folded the bill to make it look whole. But Baby Brother hadn't told me the score. He was so desperate to get drugs that he put my life in danger. And I was one of his few true friends. All he wanted was the drugs. And he knew I had a car to get him some. In the sinister world of drugs, you try to fool everybody for your habit.

The next morning, I put on my tie and went back to my job teaching school.

Losing my house and everything I had worked for should have been a rude awakening. Nearly losing my life should have been one, too. All this mind-boggling stuff was happening to me. But it was weird. For the first time in my life, I just didn't care about anything. I didn't fight back, and I didn't quit doing drugs.

I hadn't hit rock bottom yet. But at that point, I knew I was sick.

17

A Bad Trade: Super Bowl Rings for Drugs

I had this recurring dream when I was a kid:

I'm walking on train tracks through a dark tunnel. I hear a train in the distance and start running. The train starts closing in. Desperately, I run faster. But all of the sudden it's right on me. The whistle is blaring … then I'd wake up.

That's how I look at my drug problem now, from a distance of more than a decade of being clean. That dream came true. My life had been charmed. I had worked for everything I got, but I was able to overcome every obstacle. Then the drugs hit me, and I couldn't run away. I felt desperate. So helpless.

One of my lowest points came in 1983 and 1984, when I moved back to Omaha trying to kick it, to start all over. Once again, I was trying to outrun my addiction. I got a job selling cars. But I got back into drugs and soon started acting like a drug addict. But this time, it was around the people I had grown up with and loved. Seeing the pain in their eyes—and the disappointment—hurt more than any hit I took in the NFL.

The last time I had visited Omaha, I had a house. I had that Mercedes. I had a big bank account and prestige. People respected me for giving back to the community. While a player with the Dolphins, I had set up a college scholarship fund for inner-city Omaha kids.

This time I returned with no money. No car. I was not the same person.

In 1985, I thought a change of scenery might help me escape my lifestyle, so I moved back to Omaha for a year. I believed that being back home and around people who knew me to be a clean-cut, reliable, responsible person with goals and accomplishments would bring that side out of me again. I still didn't realize that only I could find that person.

I went to work for a brokerage firm in Omaha, and really believed I was on my way. I enrolled in school once again to further my business education and got an apartment right next to Nebraska-Omaha University.

But the person who had left Omaha a conquering hero was nowhere to be found. It was just I, the one who had been conquered by drugs. That devastated the people who loved me, and cared for me.

That was the year I really let everyone down and embarrassed myself. It's hard to talk about it to this day. Before I returned home that year, people had only heard about what I had become—they hadn't seen it with their own eyes, so many refused to believe it.

I brought it home to them, right in front of their eyes.

As a druggie, I didn't care. When you are on drugs, you live for the next high, not for your friends, or for yourself.

The nightlife in Omaha wasn't like L.A. But there were places I could go. One of those was a disco, which I really enjoyed. I was dancing with this woman, and I saw this guy I had grown up with, Michael Dacus. After growing up in Omaha, he had moved to Oakland, where ironically he would be my father's insurance agent.

"Hey, Marlin, sorry to hear about your father," Dacus yelled over the music.

I had no idea what he was talking about. Had his insurance lapsed? Was he in trouble?

"Sorry about what?" I asked.

"Oh, no, you didn't hear?" he said. "Your father died."

Colon cancer had claimed my father's life six months earlier. Had I not been partying and doing drugs, I would have heard about it, and been able to go to his funeral.

As it was, I had been letting drugs consume me, and I never got to say good-bye.

I was starting to slip, and very quickly, back into the world of drugs.

Again, I had a chance to get out. If I passed an exam, which I had to travel to Denver to take, I would be licensed, and I'd be able to climb the corporate ladder at my job in Omaha.

But I was out of money and needed a loan just to take the test, and get to Denver. I went to Carl Meyers, who had talked me into staying on the football team at Omaha U. when I was a freshman and Carl was our senior starting quarterback. By 1985, Carl was president of a bank in Omaha. I decided to go to him for a loan.

Carl, of course, helped me out. He knew, or had an inkling, that I had fallen onto the wrong side of the tracks. But I convinced him that I was trying to get back on my feet. I did a good selling job, and because Carl cared so much about me, he was willing to help. He secured the loan for me, but I did have to come up with some collateral, and I literally had nothing, as drugs hadn't just wiped me out emotionally and physically, but financially as well.

The ace up my sleeve was the two Super Bowl rings from the Miami Dolphins. I had put them under safeguard in Los Angeles, basically to keep me from pawning them for drug money. Since this was a legitimate loan to get back on my feet, I put them up at the bank, fully expecting to get them back as soon as I passed the exam in Denver and came back to Omaha to begin earning a good, honest living.

So I got the loan, and all my ducks were in order—finally, for the first time in ages. I just had to completely quit the drugs, which I had cut back on greatly since returning to Omaha.

I visited friends before I went to Denver. I saw the way they looked at me, either sad or angry that these drugs were running my life, and had chased away the person they knew me to be for so many years. The bottom line was that there was nowhere for me to hide in Omaha. In Los Angeles, I could disappear in an hour, and be gone for weeks, months, even years. In Omaha, everyone could see the monster that I had become, this person who was 180 degrees from the proud, upstanding, never-give-up Marlin Briscoe that had been raised there.

So I headed to the University of Denver for the license tests. As I hit Denver on Interstate 70, I saw my exit to the DU campus.

"Come on," a voice said inside of me, *"get off the road and do the right thing. Take the test."*

Another voice called out, "*Keep going man, go and go until we get to L.A., We can blend back into the world and not feel all of that guilty crap that we put up with in Omaha, what with the stares and all.*"

It was my drug habit, crying out, "*Feed me! Feed me! Don't let those bastards in Omaha kill me!*"

Honestly, I felt a physical struggle with my arms and the steering wheel, the good forces against the evil ones. The dark sea in front of me opened, and I slipped into the abyss. Though I had some money from the loan, it would quickly be gone—doesn't matter if it's $10 or $100K, a druggie will spend it all as fast as possible on drugs.

Going back to Omaha meant living two lives, one as a man masquerading as a businessman, the other as a druggie. So that day on the interstate, I kept going, all the way to Los Angeles, simply unable to go back and face my friends in Omaha. In Los Angeles, I went back to living house to house, in cars and on the street. Quickly, I was once again a street-level addict.

As I fed the beast that was my drug habit, back in Omaha in the months and years to come, Carl Meyers left the bank. And the note for my loan came due and quickly past due. Because I was out of touch and unreachable, the bank never told me that it sold my rings—as it turned out, I would be in jail when it happened. I'm still hoping to get those treasures back. That was a rude awakening as to what I had given up in my life. To be honest, I held a lot of bitterness to the people in Omaha who sold those rings. Eventually, I had to face the reality that is this: You reap what you sow. The only reason it got to the point where the rings had to be sold was because of my dereliction on the loan, and lack of direction by myself. I can't blame anyone but me for those rings being gone.

Ashamed, I went back to L.A.

I would quit for a couple months but then relapse. By 1988, I started frequenting a drug-infested area of L.A. along Washington Boulevard, an infamous area known as "Ho Stroll." "Ho" meaning "whore" in ghetto talk.

The seedy hotel rooms cost only $20 a night, $5 an hour. The police didn't care what people did inside those hotel rooms as long as it was a black-on-black situation. It wasn't until the mid-1980s, when a lot of the yuppies from downtown L.A. started coming down to get crack, that the police started to crack down on the drug and sex trade in that area.

Women of all kinds strolled that street. Black. White. Asian. Some ugly. Some nice-looking. Some, you could tell, used to be something special.

Like me.

Drug dealers stalked the street. They knew 95 percent of the prostitutes were turning tricks not for the money to take home, but for the money to take drugs. So when the women turned tricks, the money would end up with the dealers. The dealers also knew that many of the men who paid for prostitutes also would pay for drugs. So the drug dealers had everything they needed right there on "Ho Stroll."

The hotel rooms along that stretch smelled of drugs and sex. You'd go in a room and there'd be 30 people in one small room getting high. Having sex. Doing whatever drugs told them to do. In one of those rooms one time, I was sitting across from an old guy, a guy maybe in his 60s who was smoking crack. All of the sudden, he fell over and died. Nobody called an ambulance. Instead, they took his money and his crack pipe and left him lying there. They kept on doing drugs. I walked out.

I ended up living in downtown L.A. in Ho Stroll's seedy hotels and other area drug havens. To get to my room, I'd have to walk by people getting high in the hallways and stairwells. I never lived on the streets, though a few nights when I'd spent all my money on drugs, I'd have no money for rent. So I'd walk around all night, sleeping maybe a few hours propped against a wall.

Death was all around. People getting shot. People overdosing on heroin. Hearts bursting from crack. One wild woman I used to party with suddenly stopped coming to get high. I asked around, wondering where she was. No one knew or cared. A few weeks later, her chopped-up body was found in a dumpster.

Three times, I saw people shot to death over drugs. These were desperate people who had no drug money. They drove up to drug dealers standing on the street, then sped away without paying. They didn't realize that the gangsters had their lieutenants stationed at the end of the block. The gangsters would signal and the lieutenants would shoot.

It was a sinister existence. I was a duck out of water. If you're soft, you're prey. Drug dealers had a real disdain for drug users. They thought we were the lowest, weakest souls on earth because we were making them rich. They had seen again and again how drug addicts would sell their souls to get the product, even sell their girlfriends' bodies. I've seen drug dealers, especially the young gang-bangers who have no regard for anything, beat up drug addicts for no reason.

Once in a while, they'd beat me up.

Like everyone else on Ho Stroll, I had lost my self-esteem. But I always told myself that I was going to get out of that world. Those rare nights when I didn't have drugs fogging my thoughts, I'd lay awake in bed and pray, a rat or two scurrying beneath me in the dark.

Please, God let me be the person I used to be. Pull me up and out of here. Help me to overcome the demons that are inside me. Forgive me, God. Deliver me.

I remember one night about 4 o'clock along Ho Stroll; I was out looking for drugs. I was cold. I had had about two hours of sleep. The street was empty, except for this lonely figure of a man I saw across the street. Sometimes, addicts will pool money to get drugs. I had only $2.50 in my wallet. So I went over to that man. He had about $2.50, too. He recognized me.

"Aren't you Marlin Briscoe?"

Then I recognized him. He was Houston McTear, an Olympic sprinter who at one time was the fastest man in the world. Houston was in L.A. training at that time, hoping for another shot at the top. But that cold night, like me, his only goal was finding some drugs, fast. And between us, we had only enough money to buy a $5 rock of cocaine.

"It's a damned shame that it has come to this, isn't it?" I said.

"Yeah," he said, pain in his eyes.

We could barely look at each other. We were both so humiliated. Here we were, two world-class athletes, with five bucks between us. The street people knew exactly who both of us were. We had more positive history than anybody did on Ho Stroll. The street people treated us like dirt.

I had always tried to maintain my hygiene. But from 1986 to

1988, while I was living on Washington Boulevard, there were times when I would go days without a bath. I was dirty. From 1986 to 1988, I was the stereotype of a crack addict.

When I didn't have any money, no place to sleep, nothing to eat, no bus fare, I'd call a friend and he'd come get me and take me to a men's shelter near Venice Beach.

During that period, people would look at me and couldn't believe I was who I was. They could see that something was wrong with me. When you're on drugs, you can't hide it. People can see through it. I thought I was hiding it pretty well. But one day I stepped on the scale. I weighed 137 pounds. I couldn't believe it. I thought the scale was wrong. My playing weight in the NFL had been about 182 pounds. I took off my shirt and looked in a mirror.

"Wow," I said to myself. I could see my ribs. My legs were like sticks. My knees were all bony.

I realized that I wasn't the same person. I saw myself how other people saw me.

Despite all the cocaine I did, luckily I had no brain damage. No memory problems. Though I think I had brain damage at the time. My only permanent scars are from the NFL days. Even during my worst drug years, I kept working out. I'd force myself to run, even when I was weak. I'd play basketball with friends at the YMCA, even though I was slow.

When you're a drug addict, you don't care what people think. That's the evil of it. If I had cared, I would have quit right then. And when you're doing drugs, you're paranoid anyway. You're always thinking that people are thinking the worst of you.

I tried to run away from drugs. I ran to Colorado to coach. Bam! The train was there. I ran to Omaha. Bam! Still there. It was a nightmare. The only way to escape that dark tunnel was to wake up. ...

18

Tom Flores Offers Rehab

I had a chance to get clean.

Tom Flores and I crossed paths again. He allowed me to visit him at the Raiders' complex in El Segundo, California. He would loan me money, trying to help me out. One day in 1986, I saw him—as I often did—after practice. Again, he gave me some money.

"Marlin, what's going on with this?" Tom asked me.

"What do you mean?" he asked.

Tom scratched his chin and then looked me in the eye.

"Marlin, are you on drugs?" he asked me.

I was ashamed, but I could see in his eyes that he cared deeply for me.

"Marlin," Tom said. "I'm going to help you."

Flores put me up at the Raiders' hotel, the Hacienda Heights, for training camp, and put me through rehabilitation. Terry Robiske handled that program, and it really got me physically and mentally in good shape. Unfortunately, I strayed.

My car had been impounded, and Tom came through with the money for me to get my car back. I went down and picked it up, and it was in a drug neighborhood. So I fell off the wagon again instead of heading back to the rehab program.

I went to jail twice, the first time for 30 days and the second time for 90 days. The first time I went to jail was in 1988 in L.A. I walked out of a crack house and there was a flashlight in my eyes. The police had been staking out the place. They found $5 worth of cocaine on me. When I got out, I decided to make a clean start in San Diego. But soon I was back into drugs. And into jail.

The second time I went to jail was in 1990 in San Diego. This woman's car had run out of gas in the middle of a busy street. I offered to help push her car to a nearby gas station. But we pushed her car across an intersection during a red light.

She was white. The police saw us. I think they thought I was harassing her. Then the police looked over at me and saw that my eyes were all glassy and dilated.

"Can we search you?"

"Search me for what?" I asked.

They went through my briefcase and found $5 worth of crack. They also found that I had a warrant out for my arrest. After my first stint in jail, I was supposed to go through a drug diversion program. But I didn't. So the second time I went to jail, I had to stay the full 90 days.

Going to jail was the best thing that could have happened to me. Had I not gone to jail, I might still be out there, on drugs. Or dead. In jail, every night after curfew I had time to think. And every day, while I was pushing a broom or scrubbing the bathroom, I had time to think. I'd have flashbacks of the man I used to be. I'd hear the applause.

Briscoe drops to pass… He fires it off … Touchdown!

I thought about all the obstacles I had overcome, not just in athletics but in life. And here I am with a jail guard telling me to hurry up with the toilets. I'd look around me at the small cell, amid murderers, thieves and sexual deviants. Here I am, I thought, all because of a $5 piece of cocaine. Finally, I had hit rock bottom.

Finally, I started to awaken from the nightmare.

The first time I was in jail was in Los Angeles. There I had met this young white kid who was trying to earn his GED. I've always been a teacher at heart. So I tutored him. One day while I was helping the kid with algebra, this big black brother named Clark came over and told us to shut up because we were talking too loud. He couldn't hear the TV. He'd been watching cartoons.

That big buck didn't like that I was tutoring a white kid.

"If you don't quit," he said, "I'll see you when the lights go out."

I didn't quit. That guy was 6-foot-2, 240 pounds. Everybody else was afraid of him. But size never scared me. I had played football against some of the toughest and roughest players every Sunday in the NFL. I couldn't play pro football nine years and not have some violence in me. Football is a violent game.

We slept in a dormitory, about 20 guys to a room. That night after the lights went out, Clark walked over and stood next to my bottom bunk. All the other trustees were watching. The room grew tense.

Clark looked menacing. He had all these muscles from years of bench pressing while in prison. He was one of those perennial inmates, always doing time for something. At that point, he was on his way to the penitentiary. I was on my way out. I had just a few weeks of jail time left. Guys like Clark hated guys like me, the "short-timers."

"You were dissin' me today," he said.

"I told you—I was just trying to help this kid get his GED," I said. "And nobody is going to tell me not to help him. I'm not afraid of you."

"Well, then," he growled. "I'm going to kick your ass."

I got out of bed. The other inmates saw that I was not going to back down, so they broke it up before it could start. They liked me. Soon everyone went back to sleep except for me—I slept with one eye open that night.

After I got out of jail, I went to San Diego, looking for another fresh start. At first, I stayed with Dennis Shaw, who was the quarterback at Buffalo the year I made all-pro. We were the best combo in the NFL that year. Dennis lived in a real exclusive area of San Diego. I would sneak drugs into his house. He had to have an inkling of what I was doing because I kept borrowing money. I hated that, because back in our days in Buffalo, Dennis had all this confidence in me to throw to me all the time in crucial situations. And I'd come up big-time.

I had made all-pro because of him. And he had made rookie of the year because of our chemistry. And now, here I was, dropping the ball big-time.

I knew I couldn't keep sponging off him, so I got my own place.

Then the cycle of L.A. repeated itself: I moved to an apartment, then when I couldn't pay the rent, I ended up in seedy motels, then when I couldn't pay for that, I ended up in men's shelters or on the street.

One of my last jobs in San Diego was in construction. I worked for the nephew of former Dolphin teammate Nick Buoniconti. But even he had to let me go. My work fell off. I'd come in late. I'd come in high. I was always asking for advances.

When you're on the downward spiral, you have to have cheap lodgings. Cheap lodgings lead you to drug-infested areas. It was like a trap. Eventually I got busted that second time.

In the San Diego jail, I ran across this young guy I used to do drugs with. His name was Chris. He had gotten arrested two days after me. He walked in slowly, his jaw hanging down and his eyes rolling around, looking a lot like what I probably did when I walked into jail.

After a few weeks in jail, Chris totally transformed. He started working out night and day. He ate right. He slept. All of the sudden he was handsome and built, witty and smart. Any woman would have wanted him. He looked like Adonis. He even kicked my ass on the basketball court—went up over me and dunked. I couldn't believe this was the same dirty guy who had been scrounging on the street with me for drugs.

"Hey, Briscoe," he said the day he left. His eyes were shining. "This is it. I know it. I'm going to stay clean. But I need some money to help get my life together."

I loaned him $25.

Not ten days later, in walks Chris again, his jaw hanging down and his eyes rolling around. Dirty. Disoriented. He had lost all the weight he had put on. He had to have been doing drugs non-stop to lose so much weight in just 10 days.

Chris helped me realize that I couldn't just talk about staying clean. I had to walk the walk.

All those guys in jail said the same things Chris had said. *This is it. I'm going to stay clean.* But when they get out, they go right back to living in the same seedy places, hanging out with the same drugged-up crowd. Then, like Chris, they go back to drugs. I knew I couldn't go back to the same people. I knew I needed a clean environment to help me stay clean.

19

After Prison a Fresh, Clean Start

The day I left the San Diego jail, which was downtown, I held $500 in my hand. Just as I had given the $25 to Chris to help him change his life, my good friend Lance Alworth, the Hall of Fame receiver for the Chargers, had given me money to help me change my life.

"Marlin," Lance said. "This is the last time I can help you. I've always stuck by you. I can't help you anymore unless you get your life together."

I had asked a good friend from L.A., Julius Ellis, to drive down and bring me back to L.A. But Julius wouldn't arrive for a couple hours. I told him I'd wait at a hotel just a short walk from the jail.

"You know where you are," Lance said, looking toward skid row before driving off. "It's up to you, Marlin."

I looked down at the $500. Just around the corner was a crack house, one I used to go to all the time. To get to the hotel, I had to walk past that crack house and through an area infested with Cuban drug dealers. You could spot them easily. They looked like the Pied Piper, with people walking behind them to buy drugs. I used to be one of those people following behind with my $5, $10 or $20 in hand.

I started walking. I walked past a seedy hotel and saw the people I used to do drugs with. A woman I knew approached me.

"Hey, Marlin," she said, seductively. "You're sure lookin' good. Want some company? I got the bomb (the good cocaine.)"

I kept walking.

Was I tempted? Yes. I was a drug addict. I had the urge. It just doesn't go away like that. With the kind of money I had in my hand, I knew I could have stayed high a long time. Not stopping was the most difficult thing I've ever done.

That short walk through downtown San Diego was a turning point. For once, I decided to take the right turn, the right path. That short walk gave me confidence that I might just make it out.

A few hours later, my friend was driving me back to L.A.

I loved teaching almost as much as I loved playing football.

When I got out of jail in 1990, I decided to return to teaching. I still had my certificate. I had taught junior high in L.A. in 1985 and 1986. I was still productive at that point. I was popular with the kids and the faculty. But I was doing drugs. Every day I stood before those kids, I felt guilty. So I resigned.

I had a chance to get clean.

I left that teaching job—and then the rehab program—to hang out on the streets of Washington Boulevard, that place called "Ho Stroll." I did my hustle to make money. I did any job I could for drug money. I sold cars. I did telemarketing. I worked as a security guard.

When I got back to L.A., I was determined to get my life back. I moved in with Johnny Alexander, who's been my good friend since we were 9 years old. I slept on the couch.

I started substituting at a junior high school right around the corner. I was teaching math and PE Soon, I got a regular assignment as a math teacher at Morningside High School in Inglewood, California.

Things went great for three years. I stayed clean. My kids got high marks in math. I got my self-esteem back. I was one of the most popular teachers. I also got a job as an assistant coach at a junior college after school. So I was working two jobs.

I would teach mathematics at Morningside High School in the morning, and then at 3 p.m., I'd go coach football at West Los Angeles Junior College.

Morningside was a blast. We did a lot of fun things. A bunch of the girls' basketball players said they could beat me in hoops. I thought otherwise, after all I had been a standout in college, and very close to playing professional basketball for the ABA in Denver.

My competition at Morningside included Tina Thompson, who would go on to win a WNBA title with the Houston Comets. There were signs put up all over school and everything. It was a big morale boost for everyone.

When we played, Tina Thompson took me to school—there's no other way to say it. The girl just stuck it to me. Everyone at the school—even me, to be honest—enjoyed the exhibition. I developed a newfound respect for women's basketball.

Coaching football was also a lot of fun. It got me back into the sport, but not to the degree that it would consume me. My first year coaching at West L.A. was 1991, and I coached Isaac Bruce, who was just a great young man. I loved him like a son. He was at junior college to get his grades up so he could go play Division I-A football at a four-year college.

In 1992, Keyshawn Johnson joined our team. Keyshawn was tremendously talented, and the most difficult player I ever encountered. We quickly developed a deep rift. He and I disagreed completely about his approach to practice.

Keyshawn was actually a great defensive back, and we wanted him to play both ways. He could have revolutionized the position of cornerback, being as big and strong as he is, yet having great speed and a nose for making plays.

We were running a wishbone offense—yet we had two of the greatest receivers in the country. Isaac had enough, and transferred to a junior college in Santa Monica. I had enough of Keyshawn, and he had enough of me, so Keyshawn quit the team.

A lot of people had enough of Keyshawn, but the coaches knew he had talent, and they wanted to keep a good relationship with his high school. I saw the writing on the wall.

I felt the coaches let Keyshawn get away with too much. Keyshawn wanted to always do things his own way. He'd go through practice at defensive back, and then come to work with the receivers and me.

Keyshawn just wouldn't listen. Though I had other receivers who worked hard—and were very good—the coaches would push Keyshawn as the starter for games. I felt like that sent the wrong message to the guys who worked hard, and sacrificed for the team—who weren't just in it for themselves. I had never seen any kid like that—it was just unreal.

I still loved teaching, and coaching, though coaching at West L.A. was no longer the right situation for me.

Then one morning at Morningside as I was preparing for the day, a substitute teacher walks into my classroom.

"Mr. Briscoe," he said. "I'm taking over your class."

"What are you talking about?"

"You're supposed to go to the office."

The principal said that I had a problem with my teaching credential and that I had to go to the district office. People at the district office said there was inquiry into my credential and that I couldn't teach until it was cleared up.

Turns out that because I had gone to jail on a drug conviction, all of the sudden the state wouldn't allow me to teach. Later that day, I told the head coach at the junior college what had happened to me.

"You know you can't teach here either," he said. "The state controls us, too."

The next year, Keyshawn would rejoin the team, and I was out of the picture.

I ended up going to a University of Southern California game against the University of Houston several years later. I stood with Kellen Winslow, the great tight end for San Diego. Keyshawn, who was playing for USC, had done some growing up and came over to me as Kellen and I watched the game from the field.

"Sorry for any problems I caused you," Keyshawn said, and he hugged me.

I thought that was a nice gesture; don't get me wrong. But I still think Isaac Bruce was the better all-around player, no doubt about it.

At the moment I lost my teaching job, I was stunned. It was an all-time low. In one day, I had lost two jobs. I had told the truth on my job application. I had written down the dates I was in jail and the reasons. For three years, it never came up.

The Inglewood school district had been having widespread problems with theft and graft. Even a high-level administrator was accused of stealing money. A janitor had been caught stealing money through school computers. So the state started investigating every employee.

I had made it through 10 years of pure hell, being down and out and not doing the right thing, not doing my true calling—which is teaching and coaching—and I had lost everything. And then after three years of doing the right thing and staying clean...

Bam.

I was on the verge of just going ahead and getting high. Heck with it all. The only reason I didn't was because I was taking care of a little boy, my ex-girlfriend's boy. He was like a son to me.

One day while I was still working at Morningside, I found out that my girlfriend was doing drugs behind my back. I asked her to move out. She did. She went off and became a full-blown addict. But she left her 10-year-old boy behind with me. He was like my son. He kept me sane. He saved me from going back to drugs.

I lost my two jobs a few days before Thanksgiving. My ex-girlfriend phoned me and asked if she could come over and cook a turkey dinner for the boy and me. She said she wanted to have the "family" back together. She told me she had quit doing drugs.

I had a little house I was renting. She came over and fixed a real nice dinner. Afterwards, the boy went outside to play and my ex-girlfriend and I were alone.

"Come up in the bedroom," she said alluringly.

My ex-girlfriend was beautiful and talented. Before she had turned to drugs, she had been a professional singer and a nurse.

We walked to bedroom. She shut the door. I thought we were about to rekindle a relationship, and hopefully this one would be healthy, for both of us.

She reached down, and pulled out some sacks of cocaine and a pipe.

I looked at it. I reached out for it. I thought about losing my jobs.

Then I realized she was trying to get me back by dragging me back into that downward spiral. And once you do drugs one time, that's it. You're back on it.

"You have to go," I said, and left the room quickly.

She wouldn't leave. So I phoned my friend Julius Ellis and told him what was happening.

"Hey, man," I said. "You got to get me out of here."

He came right away.

The easiest way for a man—a weak man, at least—to get back on drugs is through a woman who is on drugs. Each time I relapsed, it was through a woman who did drugs. Over the years, I saw a lot of men return to drugs that way. That's not to blame the woman, because I made my own choices, as did the other guys who went back to drugs the same way.

My ex-girlfriend went back to her drug life and her hotel room above a seedy bar. It was sad to see a woman so beautiful, funny and witty so drugged out. She's OK now, thank goodness. Like me, she had to hit rock bottom before she could pull herself back up. She's clean now and married to a decent guy.

You can't judge people as bad just because they do drugs. But drugs will make you do bad things. That ex-girlfriend was a lovely woman. But she wasn't herself when she was high. A lot of the women I met on Ho Stroll, when they were clean, they looked like the kind of girls you'd take home to your mama.

I'm very lucky to have escaped the drug scene without contracting a sexually transmitted disease. I know some people who weren't so lucky, who got AIDS and died. As a drug addict, you find yourself in the company of strange women all the time. They're only with you because you have drugs. They'll do anything for you for drugs. And you know that if they've done it for you, they've done it for someone else.

That Thanksgiving, I knew that if I took even one puff of that pipe, I'd be back in that world. I realized that I had a lot to be thankful for. God had given me a second chance. And he had more lessons for me to learn.

After I lost my teaching job, Morningside High School gave me another job running an after-school program for at-risk kids. But it was at a lot less money. And I was on campus every day.

"Mr. Briscoe," my old students would ask. "Why aren't you in class anymore?"

I couldn't tell them why. I couldn't take it anymore. So I took other jobs to survive. But my heart wasn't in them. I was defeated.

After a period of feeling sorry for myself, I decided to shape up. I told myself, "Hey, it may not be fair. But this is a result of what you did, your own bad decisions."

I got a job selling tools.

Sometimes I wake up in a cold sweat thinking about what I've lost because of drugs. To be so stupid to let drugs control me is mind-boggling to me now. I hate the fact that I used my friends for drug money. That I used my good name. My friends gave me money at first because they knew the guy I was before the drugs took over. They were hoping that I would snap out of it. But you can't snap out of it easily, regardless of your background.

I alienated many friends. They soon realized they were hurting me more than helping me by giving me the means to buy drugs. That's why I went out and did my "little hustle" around L.A. I go to those same areas now, and I remember how I used to play games with people.

The year after I was named all-pro, I met this gorgeous black woman named Kathleen Bradley at a birthday party for Muhammad Ali. She was the talk of the party, just stunningly beautiful. She had come to the party with Al Cowlings, O.J.'s friend whom later chauffeured Simpson on that famous white Bronco chase.

We talked a long time that night. Then we started dating. I think she liked the fact that instead of chasing her like every other man, I had been brash with her. She was a nice lady. We had a lot in common. I was the first black quarterback in the NFL. She was the first black woman on "The Price Is Right" TV game show.

We stayed good friends after we dated. She and some girl-friends had formed a singing group called the Love Machine. When I was playing for Miami, they'd stay with me when they were in town. Guys on the team used to joke that I had my own harem. But we were just friends.

One day, years later, I was standing on a corner in South Central L.A and Kathleen drove by in a convertible.

"Hey, Kathy," I yelled. She stopped, not recognizing me.

"It's me, Marlin. I need a ride. My car's broken down."

She knew I was out of it. She didn't say much. I could tell she was disappointed in me. Then I asked to borrow some money.

Years later—not long ago, in fact—I saw Kathleen again at the funeral of our mutual friend, Tody Smith, who used to play for the Dallas Cowboys and the Houston Oilers. Kathleen came up and gave me a big hug.

"You look so good now," she said, smiling. "I'm so happy you've got your life back."

I hear those comments a lot now. Friends have faith in me again. When I look in their eyes, I can see the old me. I can see that they see the old me, too. But I know I can't get cocky again.

I know I must always keep my guard up so I'm not blindsided again.

Recently, I ran into another gorgeous woman from my past—I'll call her Jane—the woman who had cooked up my first taste of free-base cocaine that day in my house with the pool. I ran into her at the convenience store just around the corner from my daughter Becky's grandparents' house in L.A.

I pulled up in a Mercedes convertible, just like the one I used to own, only this one is white. I had always promised myself, when I had to sell that first tan Mercedes, that one day I'd get another one just like it.

"You're looking good," she said. She didn't look good. She looked too thin. She looked like she was still doing drugs.

"I see you got your car back," she said. "I'm so happy for you. I always knew you'd make it out."

She said that she was living with a man and that he was out of town.

"Bye, Jane," I said, and then drove away fast. When I got home that night, I heard Jane's voice on the answering machine, though I hadn't even given her my phone number.

"Hey, Marlin," she said. "Why don't you take me to dinner? And then maybe we could party."

I erased the message.

20

The O.J. Simpson Murder Trial

In 1994, a year after losing my job as a teacher and coach, life kicked me hard again. First, I developed an enlarged prostate. The doctor thought I might have cancer. He said I needed surgery. I was in terrible pain. And then O.J. got arrested for murder in the death of his ex-wife, Nicole. I was close to both of them.

Days before surgery, I was lying on my couch talking on the phone to a lady friend. I had been in so much pain I hadn't been paying attention to the news. The TV was on in the background, but the sound was off. I saw O.J. on the TV screen, and he was wearing handcuffs.

"Oh, look," I told my lady friend. "O.J.'s in another movie. It's amazing—it looks so real."

"You fool," she said. "It is live. O.J. got arrested for murdering his wife and another person."

I was devastated. I couldn't believe it. Not Nicole. Just weeks before, I had been talking with Nicole. Not O.J. Not the O.J. I knew and loved. The guy who'd do anything for a friend.

Before surgery, I had to wear a catheter. I couldn't walk and I couldn't work, so I had no money.

But I needed prescription drugs, which were very expensive. I called up O.J.'s house to borrow some money. A woman answered the phone. It was Nicole.

"Hey, Marlin," she said. "How are you doing? O.J.'s in New York right now." I had known Nicole from all the times I had played basketball at O.J.'s house in Brentwood. She'd bring us out snacks and cold drinks. She was sweet. I told her about my prostate problem. She phoned O.J. right away, and then O.J. called a pharmacy in Brentwood and arranged to pay for any medications I needed.

That's the O.J. I knew a generous guy who'd do anything for a friend. Even though they were divorced, he and Nicole still seemed close.

Nicole's death, O.J.'s Bronco flight, the trial. My life had been full of drama up to that point. But the story that unfolded over the next year was a drama even I couldn't believe. A drama with a surreal plot. I wished it all had been just a movie starring O.J, and that the lovely, wonderful Nicole was alive and well.

During O.J.'s trial, I frequented an Italian restaurant owned by an ex-NFL player in Hollywood. On my birthday that September, I had gone over to my mother's house and she had given me all these old pictures from my playing days. There were a lot of pictures of O.J. and me together. He and I playing football. He and I socializing.

Later that day at that restaurant, I'm at the bar telling the owner all the stories about O.J and me. I noticed two guys next to me listening real intently.

"You've got some real interesting stories about O.J.," one of them said.

"Yeah, he's one of my best friends."

"I can see that," he said. "We're part of his defense team. And we're here from New York with the TV show 'A Current Affair' to cover the O.J. trial.

"How would you like to go on 'A Current Affair' and tell your story?"

I told them there was no way I'd be part of a story that would taint the case. They assured me that they wanted to present his human side to the public.

"A Current Affair" was a big TV tabloid at the time. A producer arranged to meet with me a few days later, and she liked what I said and how I presented myself. The people with the show did all this research on me and learned all I had done in the NFL. They learned that I had been a pioneer for black quarterbacks. The segment turned out to be more about me than O.J.

I noticed a resurgence of interest in me after that segment ran. The national media picked up on it and I started getting interviewed a lot. Before that, I had become a lost chapter in NFL history.

Here's another memory: After my last year at Buffalo, when I had just returned from Vietnam with the Bob Hope show I was staying in L.A. working at my summer job. I lived in an apartment across from the Hollywood Park racetrack. This was right after I was traded to Miami.

I was training one day, riding my bicycle, when a silver Lincoln Continental pulled up alongside me on the street.

"Hey, nigger, get out of the (expletive) street!"

I hate that word. I always have, and always will. It symbolizes ignorance and hate.

I looked over. Behind the wheel was a young white man. I glared at him, but kept riding. From where he was sitting, I couldn't imagine that it was his voice I was hearing.

"Yeah, that's me," the voice continued. "I said it, nigger."

Really angry at that point, I turned to say a few words to the man. Then I heard a familiar laugh and saw this big old familiar large head rise up from the passenger side. It was O.J. He was laughing. O.J. had decided to play a little prank on me.

I put my bike in the car and we went on to the Hollywood Park to bet on O.J.'s horse—which lost.

The white guy driving the Lincoln Continental? That was O.J.'s good friend, the lawyer who later became famous as a member of O.J.'s defense team, Robert Kardashian, who had been close to both O.J. and Nicole.

I am asked time and again if I think O.J. did it. The answer is, I don't know.

I don't know who killed Nicole and her friend. I do know, from hearing logistics reports done long after the murders, that it likely took at least two people, and that one of them was left-handed—that was determined from the fatal knife wound on one of the victims.

Was one of those O.J.? I can't say either way because I don't know. I do know, from first-hand experience, that the police in Southern California are not beyond reproach in their attitude, and investigation methods. Does that mean O.J. didn't do it? I don't know. I do know the investigation was flawed, and that there was a racist element to it, part of which was on display as the case played out in court.

The bottom line is this: I knew the O.J. Simpson who was one of America's favorite athletes and pitch-men in the 1970s and 1980s and as an actor. I didn't see a violent side to him or the much-talked about temper. I do know that O.J. helped me out, as a friend, when I needed it most.

As far as anything else goes, though, I can't make a judgment. And it's not really my place, either. I was close to O.J. and Nicole, and cared greatly for both.

That's really all I can say about the tragic, sad matter. And whoever did kill her deserves whatever they get.

21

"1-0"

Every day since I emerged from the darkness of drugs is another challenge, another opportunity to move forward.

I'm not known as "17-0" any longer. Instead, I try to be "1-0"—making it through each day, and looking forward to making the best of each and every day. One day at a time. Then I get up the next morning. Start over. Finish that day 1-0. And so on.

That means staying away from drugs, and sharing my experience with others going through what I did. At the same time, it means going to schools and youth centers to help young people avoid the mistakes I made. In this society, we have rehabilitation for everything. What we need more of is pre-emptive intervention, a "pre-habilitation" if you will.

For me, a big part of the solution was faith, the very thing that lifted me to the lofty goals as a player and person before I began my slide. I prayed every day as a drug addict, "God, help me through this nightmare." I did the same thing when I went to jail. And I realized many prisoners in there were praying, and finding God. That's a good thing, don't get me wrong. But if we had maintained or developed our faith before we created our problems, we wouldn't have found ourselves in jail in the first place. And that's something that just can't go unsaid.

As soon as I got back out of jail, I remembered how I had counted on God, and I had to make sure God knew He could count on me. To that end, First Presbyterian, the church I now attend in Southern California, became a pivotal part of my recovery. When I got out of jail, I became actively involved in every facet of the church.

There are many wonderful people at my church. The late Delores Wilson, who went to God's side after Lupus claimed her life in 1998, helped me re-establish my umbilical cord to God. I owe a lot to her. When I left jail in San Diego, she was the first one to serve as my spiritual mentor, a real life angel. Without her helping me, I might have relapsed. She helped me get my spiritual strength back, and establish a Christian support system.

Wayne Hawkins, the church pastor, and Ruth Hirshman also helped me greatly. First Presbyterian is one of the spiritual cornerstones in Ingewood history, and I was blessed to join that family.

I went to Bethel Baptist Church in Omaha. That's a different denomination, obviously, but the important thing is to connect with God, regardless of the religious affiliation. I enjoy reading the Bible on my own. So many organizations have different interpretations of the Bible. The important thing is to build your own relationship with God, one that you can understand and nurture.

As an educator, I've seen how prayer has been taken out of the schools through the last half of the 20th Century. The courts have taken that away from kids in school. Because of those decisions, there has been a lot of degradation of the school experience. We've had school shootings and all kinds of other violence in schools. Yet what is the first thing school and civic officials do when we have that kind of school violence?

They pray, even publicly, and ask others to pray for their school and kids.

Why did we ever stop in the first place?

If kids were taught the principles of everyone being equal, treating others as you'd like to be treated, and so on, many of these incidents would have never happened because young people would have that solid foundation in place, and they'd know right from wrong.

I think it's a shame that many only turn to God during adversity. As long as we're free and things are going well, many have no use for the Bible and God, following their own selfish agenda and ideology.

No one has to subscribe to my own personal Christian beliefs, or go to the same church or belong to the same religion. But it is important to have your own faith, and to adhere to it. When we stray from that path, the obstacles pop up, and those without faith don't respond morally.

22

The Changing Landscape of the NFL

I basically put my career in jeopardy by my union activities, which were geared to try and get a better pension plan. A key player in that was attorney Ed Garvey, whom I called "Wally Cox."

Wally Cox was a demure, funny looking guy with glasses who was on a television show, Mr. Peepers, back in the 1950s, and looked just like Ed Garvey.

Ed was a tenacious negotiator, and very stubborn to help our cause. He also handled the Rozelle Rule lawsuit. Back in those days, players couldn't get the pension until age 65. And there were no survivor benefits in place in case a player died—the family didn't get the benefits; it went back into the owners' pool.

We, the union, had an actuary—a study, basically—done that showed the average player during our era would die at age 53. So most players wouldn't collect a dime on the pension. It took a five-year career in the league to get a pension, yet the average career was only a little more than three years, about 3.2 years at that time.

Now it takes a four-year career to qualify for the pension. But the average player still only plays about 3.6 years.

I opted to take my pension at 45, even though the benefits are reduced greatly if the pension is taken at that age. At 55, the benefits are more, but still reduced from what they would be if the player waits until 65.

At age 45 I drew $336 a month pension from the NFL. In the

NBA, Major League Baseball and other pro leagues—even two decades ago—players were getting thousands of dollars a month.

My pension has since increased twice, once to $476 a month, and then to $720 a month, which it remains to this day—for nine years of service to the league.

Pro football generates more revenue than any sport. But the injuries we sustain are more severe than any other sport.

We set the tone for these players today getting these huge salaries. Take my entire retirement and it wouldn't equal one game check for the players today. With the millions the players are making today, they're not worried about pension plan. When I came into the league, the minimum salary was $12,500, and now it is $350,000. When I played we worked in the off-season or enrolled in school so we could have a decent job when our careers ended.

At the height of my drug problem, I needed rehabilitation. I called the league and player association offices.

"Can I get help for drug rehabilitation?" I asked. "I need to be in a program."

"Sure, but we need $8,000 first," I was told.

"If I had $8,000, I wouldn't need to be calling you," I answered.

It's humiliating to call. We're often treated rudely, as though we're a nuisance, or that we don't exist.

These feelings are certainly by no means limited to me. Most players of our era were totally overlooked. The guys who played before us, like Red Grange, Bronko Nagurski and Jim Brown were overlooked even more. Even guys like Johnny Unitas have tried to get changes in the pension plan.

I'm not resentful of the guys today earning the money they do—I would have taken it, too—but I don't think the guys who sacrificed to get the game to where it is today should be overlooked.

The injuries we sustained as players creep up on us later in life. So it was better to take disability from a financial standpoint, instead of the pension.

As we grow older, players need disability more than pension because of their medical bills. Their medical problems from their football careers weren't as serious when they were 45 and they took the pension.

And once they signed for that pension, they forfeited the disability option. I think that rule should change. I know personally that when you hit your 50s, those injuries that you sustained when you were younger are much more serious, so much so it's hard to get out of bed, much less earn a decent living.

The landscape of the NFL is changing. Though there are still steps backward in terms of hiring minorities for coaching and front office positions, the black quarterback has made great strides. No longer is it a widely held belief that blacks aren't smart enough to play quarterback.

So I feel a sense of pride seeing the guys today. I can't take full credit for it, but I was one of the pioneers. A lot of the black quarterbacks coming up today didn't know the history of what we—myself, James Harris, Dickey and Gilliam—went through to make this path. If they did, they would be able to appreciate the sacrifice, and even anticipate better some challenges they might face.

I met Rodney Peete, who had an outstanding career at the University of Southern California before having an unspectacular NFL career with a myriad of teams. Someone tried to introduce me to Rodney, and he turned his back on me, and walked away. I thought that was very disrespectful.

But there are quarterbacks who understand, and appreciate, what we went through. Doug Williams was a great role model, and player. Warren Moon is a great example. Ditto for Kordell Stewart, Donovan McNabb, Daunte Culpepper and many, many others who are playing now.

One of the most pleasant interactions for me was in September 2001, in Buffalo. Aaron Brooks, the black quarterback for New Orleans, had just thrown three touchdown passes against the Bills. Yet he came over to see me, and knew all about my story, and what I had experienced. He was very educated about the history of the black quarterback, and he shook my hand, thanking me for what I did.

Those kinds of things mean a lot.

I've been working with young people since I took my life back. I worked as a dean at a private school, and I've worked since 1997 with a youth center in Watts. The time with the kids means everything to me.

I tell them what I've been through, and I explain to them the need for personal accountability, and responsibility, and how it is more important than ever in this day and age.

My life has been a lot of triumphs over adversity. The biggest triumph—aside from faith and family—that I'm most proud of, is overcoming the hideous drug addiction. My story just shows you that no matter how much success you have, life is not a continuum; that is, the more success you have, the more opportunities you have to stray away from who you are because your life expands. No matter what happens to you, keep life as simple as possible. Never forget who you are. Because when success spoils you, it will bite you if your foundation isn't solid—and sometimes, even if it is solid.

My story also shows that you can overcome anything. If you are strong-minded, you can overcome the dark side of life and remain in the positive light.

There have been bumps in the road, and things I'd do differently if I could do them over again. By sharing my story, I know I can influence kids in a positive way, that they can reach for the stars, and chase their dreams while being good citizens, and eventually responsible adults.

We still live in the greatest country in the world. The events of September 11, 2001, show us that there are still people who want to take away freedom, happiness and the ability to choose what we do in life.

But if we lean on each other, and our faith, we will prevail. And by doing so, we will make the world a better place for everyone.